SMUGGLERS OF THE WEST

Tales of Contraband and Crooks

ROSEMARY NEERING

VICTORIA · VANCOUVER · CALGARY

Heritage House Publishing Company Ltd.
www.heritagehouse.ca

Library and Archives Canada Cataloguing in Publication
Neering, Rosemary, 1945–
Smugglers of the west: tales of contraband and crooks / Rosemary Neering.

(Amazing stories)
Includes bibliographical references and index.
Issued also in an electronic format.
ISBN 978-1-926936-91-8

1. Smugglers—Canada—Biography. 2. Smuggling—Canada—History. 3. Canada, Western—History. I. Title. II. Series: Amazing stories (Victoria, B.C.)

FC3217.1.N44 2011   364.1'3309711   C2011-905041-2

Series editor: Lesley Reynolds
Proofreader: Liesbeth Leatherbarrow
Cover design: Chyla Cardinal. Interior design: Frances Hunter.
Cover photo: oneclearvision/iStockphoto.com

The interior of this book was produced on 100% post-consumer recycled paper, processed chlorine free and printed with vegetable-based inks.

Heritage House acknowledges the financial support for its publishing program from the Government of Canada through the Canada Book Fund (CBF), Canada Council for the Arts and the province of British Columbia through the British Columbia Arts Council and the Book Publishing Tax Credit.

 Canadian Patrimoine Heritage canadien   Canada Council Conseil des Arts for the Arts du Canada   BRITISH COLUMBIA ARTS COUNCIL

Printed in Canada

15 14 13 12 11   1 2 3 4 5

Contents

Prologue

UNDER COVER OF NIGHT, *a Japanese schooner ghosted along the coast of Vancouver Island, northwest of Victoria. The ship's boats were lowered. Seventy-eight men clambered down and rowed to shore with packs containing tinned meat, army biscuits, tents and hammocks. The boats then returned silently to the schooner.*

At first light, the men—many of them dressed in army uniforms from the Russo-Japanese War that had ended the year before—consulted maps, shouldered packs and formed into military-style columns. They strode from the beach into the forest and began their trek.

They had spent seven weeks at sea before arriving in Canada as smuggled immigrants. Their task now was to march overland, avoiding contact with Vancouver Island residents as much as possible. At Sidney, some 50 kilometres away by a direct route, many more by the roundabout route that they had been instructed to follow, a steamer would meet them to take them clandestinely to the Fraser Valley, where work awaited.

There was no time to waste. As silently as they could, they moved through the forest, setting up bivouacs at night, then forging ahead as soon as the light allowed. Not everyone was robust enough for the march, but the fittest could not wait for the weary. One by one or in groups, those who could not keep up with the rest of the column were left behind. The others continued on, always checking their detailed maps.

What did they make of this new land, so different from Japan and so sparsely settled? We do not know. We do know that after a march of several days, just 26 of the original 78 emerged from the trees and meadows of the Saanich Peninsula to seek the ship that would take them to safety. No ship awaited them. Like many other smugglers' voyages, this one did not go according to plan.

Introduction

ON EITHER SIDE OF Juan de Fuca Strait lie dozens of islands, coves, bays and crooked waterways. Draw through these geographic features an arbitrary line that defines the border between Canada and the United States. Continue this boundary by way of a straight line along a parallel of latitude that stops for no chain of mountains, lake or river, through territory that for the 19th and much of the 20th century was scantily populated.

It was a smuggler's paradise.

In the 21st century, illegal immigrants reach the west coast of Vancouver Island aboard ships that come from Asia. Huge caches of marijuana are stealthily smuggled south, or heroin and cocaine move undetected into British

Columbia by plane, truck or ship. On another level, we smile at customs officers at the border and hope they don't look closely at the trunk of our car and find the undeclared goods that we are bringing in from the United States. And we think we have come upon something new, whether it is large-scale smuggling of contraband or trifling evasion of taxes.

Yet smuggling across the border between British Columbia and the United States is a long tradition, one that began almost the moment two countries drew a line that said, "This is ours, and that is yours." In the 1850s and 1860s, wool and gold went south illegally, without duty being paid, and miners' packs and cattle came north. For almost 30 years from the 1880s on, smoking opium, legally manufactured in Victoria and Vancouver, was spirited across the border to dodge the heavy duty that was imposed on legal imports of the drug. Once opium was made illegal in both countries, smuggling continued both ways across the Canada–United States border. At the same time, hundreds of Chinese labourers were smuggled south, by stealth or by fraud, to start a new life in the United States.

Fifteen years after opium was prohibited, small boats once more stole through the straits and Puget Sound, seeking the pinpoint of light ashore that marked the drop-off point for the cargo of liquor that they carried. Down the coast, large ships that sailed from Vancouver and Victoria stood in international waters on Rum Row, delivering

8

cases of whisky and rum to small boats that then dashed for American shores with their smuggled cargo. Further inland, liquor moved by car, train, raft and even horse from the border towns of British Columbia to thirsty Americans in Washington, Idaho and Montana.

Here on the map is a Smugglers' Cove; there lies a Smugglers Bay. The names commemorate the illegal movement of goods across the line. Most early smugglers were simply intent on evading duties imposed by protectionist regimes on either side of the line. Professionals smuggled to sell, amateurs for their own personal use. A Victorian lady might tuck fashionable clothes sent out from England under her skirts when she returned from Victoria to Port Townsend. A man about town might conceal a box of cigars or cigarettes when he came back from a visit to Seattle. The professionals dealt in larger quantities, smuggling a great variety of items that were legal in both countries, but subject to duty the moment they crossed the border. The professionals dealt also in what was legal in one country but illegal in the other and, on occasion, what was illegal in both.

Whatever the cargo, whatever the route, from the day the border was drawn on a map, smuggling between the two countries thrived.

1

In the Beginning

SHUFFLING ALONG THE NARROW TRAIL, the prospector shifted his heavy pack to a more comfortable position. Up ahead, he knew from talking to like-minded men, lay the border between the Oregon Territory and the newly named colony of British Columbia. He knew, too, what to expect when he arrived at the border, but he had no intention of letting it happen to him. "By God, and by my rights as an American," he growled to himself, "I'm not paying any duties on my gear. They can whistle for their money. I'll wait till dark and slip across the border when they're sleeping. I'll be miles away before the customs man even wakes up."

The story is apocryphal, but it represents many a man who headed north for the various gold rushes in British

Columbia from 1858 on. One of the first things Governor James Douglas did after assuming the post of governor of the mainland colony was to set customs duties on anything imported into the region. How else, he and other colonial officials asked, could the colony afford to build roads and keep the law? As one official wrote to the colonial secretary in London, expenses such as these could be paid by "a small *ad valorem* duty on British imports, with an increase upon foreign imports, &," suggesting a policy that would always be popular with governments, "a considerable augmentation on ardent spirits in proportion to their proof. No revenue could be raised sufficient for present purposes, by any other means so readily . . . and at so small an expense to the mother country."

With the first customs duties came the first smugglers. Though Victoria was a free port for a few years from 1860 on, no such benefits accrued to New Westminster and other mainland points, and gold rushers who came by land preferred to evade duties whenever they could. In his 1887 history of British Columbia, Hubert Howe Bancroft reported the result:

> Smuggling was practised largely from the first appearance of the gold fever. Particularly along the United States border it was found impossible, where all was hurry and helter-skelter, and goods were carried on men's backs as well as by horses and canoes, to prevent large quantities of merchandise from passing the line untaxed. So great became this contraband

traffic that a serious commercial depression which prevailed at New Westminster in the winter of 1860–1 was charged directly to it.

In 1859, two American soldiers escaped pursuing Natives by scuttling north across the border in the country east of present-day Osoyoos, where they chanced upon gold in the Kettle River. Soon, some 5,000 prospectors were streaming north, and not one of them was paying duty on the goods and supplies he carried. James Douglas added a second customs officer to the area, "for restraining the illicit importation of goods into British Columbia," but it was to no avail. "It is, however, impossible, I conceive," wrote Douglas, "altogether to prevent smuggling at places situated so immediately on the frontier as Rock Creek." As a Portland newspaper noted in December 1860, in a report from Rock Creek:

> The British officials here are having a lively time at present, in attempting to prevent goods being smuggled into British territory. The boundary line is only three miles from here and two trains are just outside awaiting a favorable opportunity to run their goods in and avoid paying the ten per cent duty on dry goods and groceries and $1.50 a gallon on liquors. Another dodge is to take all the goods across the line upon the same horse, thereby saving $1.50 on each horse, that being the duty on every animal taken into British territory.

In the Beginning

The bust of the Rock Creek boom seems to have slowed things down, however, as did the stationing of yet another customs officer on the border. But stories abound of the smuggling of everything in the region, from gold to donkeys, horses and flour.

Prospectors weren't the only ones to object to the duties. Merchants who tried to make their living honestly were faced with smuggled goods that sold much more cheaply. "We have to pay duty for importing live cattle, and potatoes are also taxed," complained one such merchant, reported in the Victoria *British Colonist* on July 4, 1859. "A heavy duty is paid on spirits, which is quite right if smuggling is to be prevented, but as I know that 900 gallons were smuggled in last week, what chance has the honest merchant?"

Smuggling went both ways. A heavy tax was imposed on gold taken out of the colony; many miners used whatever stratagems they could to evade it. In the 1860s, the prospectors at Wild Horse Creek in the East Kootenays—and their friends—were inventive. According to local tales, the female proprietor of the Roosville store, who packed goods north across the border to the British Columbia mining camps, was happy to help out a man in need. On her way south, she would smuggle nuggets across the border for a fee, presumably hiding them somewhere in her clothes. Rock Creek miners were said to move south with their gold on moonless nights, when they could be more certain of evading the authorities.

The list of goods smuggled in the early days of British Columbia was a long one, and it was far from a one-way street. According to the *Colonist*, American ladies on the San Juan Islands yearned after the superior quality of the British-made ladies' wear available in Victoria. The editorialist opined:

> It is only natural that such establishments as we have here—for instance, the London House, the Victoria House, the Hudson's Bay Company's great emporium and the Messrs' Wilson and Gray's establishments—will draw more or less custom from neighbouring communities.
>
> The splendid array of rich and fashionable French and English goods at prices which are in such astounding contrast with those on the other side must be quite irresistible to the ladies of Puget Sound.

American customs officials were so annoyed at such smuggling that they decided to put a stop to it. They hired a female customs inspector to travel the boats that plied between Washington ports and Victoria. It was claimed that almost all the passengers on the boats had previously been female, but after the inspector went to work, said the *Colonist* reporter, there were almost no women aboard. "Our contemporary [in Washington State] does not hesitate to attribute this change to the presence of the Argus-eyed 'female inspector of customs,' intimating that quite an extensive smuggling trade was carried on by the fair sex."

But, suggested the paper, perhaps it was simply not the right time of year for smuggling.

On the mainland, smoking opium was smuggled south to Chinese miners at work on the diggings on the Columbia River near Colville. The Portland *Oregonian* was aghast. "This lucrative trade is encouraged by the absence of any force in the section of country where the trails from British Columbia cross the boundary. There are also circumstances which give rise to the belief that illicit traffic between British Columbia and other parts of the upper country is carried on; the articles being jewelry, laces and the like."

Then, as now, the variety of smuggled goods was considerable. One report tells of a sailor who tried to smuggle cloth off a British Navy ship for sale in Victoria. Another reveals that in 1861, 124 pieces of ribbon were smuggled into San Francisco from a ship that had begun its journey in Victoria. No further detail is given, except to note that the purported owner of the ribbon did not appear in court to reclaim his prize.

Much of the smuggling involved traffic between Victoria and the San Juan Islands. And why not, asked the residents of those islands? As evidenced by their belligerence in what became the Pig War, the islands' early settlers were highly independent and resistant to government authority. As far as they were concerned, smuggling was neither a crime nor a sin, but simply good business. "Smuggling is a species of law-breaking over which the Ten Commandments have no jurisdiction," is an oft-repeated piece of wisdom attributed to island residents.

The thrifty islanders kept a close watch on prices in their islands and in British territory. From the 1860s through the 1890s, sheep's wool was 20 cents a pound cheaper on the Gulf Islands and Vancouver Island than it was in the American territories. Add in the duty on wool imports, however, and the price difference was tiny. But why add in that duty, asked the islanders, when wool was wool, and its origin impossible to identify? Very little wool actually passed through American customs houses, yet the amount that left the San Juans vastly exceeded the amount that the island flocks of sheep could produce. Wool smuggling persisted, and it was not until 1905 that authorities found an answer to the practice.

The smuggling of liquor south during Prohibition is well known, but it comes from a long tradition. In 1866, a great foofaraw erupted in Victoria and points south over the purported involvement of a ship's crew and captain in smuggling liquor south aboard the ship *Sir James Douglas*. The ship's captain testified that a Mr. Lyons had asked him in Victoria if he would help him out by taking liquor across to the United States. Not a chance, the captain claimed he had replied; the only way he knew of to take liquor south on the *Douglas* was by clearing customs.

Based on the infamous "information received," American officials descended on the ship when it arrived in

Bellingham Bay. With the full co-operation of the captain and at least some of the crew, they searched the ship. Nothing was found. It must be somewhere, said the US Customs men. They searched again, more carefully, and discovered liquor in the forecastle. Evidence linked Lyons to the cache. He was charged and quickly tried, but found not guilty for want of sufficient evidence. The captain was exonerated.

2

Fuelling the
Heavenly Habit

THE SMELL OF BOILING POTATOES spilled into the narrow confines of the courtyards and alleys of Victoria's Chinatown. The click of mah-jong tiles and fantan beads echoed past the hurrying footsteps of men who slipped through doorways and up wooden staircases. The smell, the sounds, the movement were all familiar to anyone who wandered into the half-dozen city blocks in the 1880s and for several decades thereafter. The smell was not in fact potatoes but the odour of smoking opium being produced from the sticky, dark brown balls of raw opium that arrived by ship from India. Smoking opium was much desired by the Chinese immigrants who had come here for the gold rush, for the building of the Canadian Pacific Railway (CPR) or for many other jobs not as willingly or as cheaply done by European immigrants.

It was hard to hide the smell, especially since about 15 small factories were located in and around the area, each engaged in refining raw opium. But at that time there was no need to hide. Importing, refining, using and exporting opium were perfectly legal in Canada, provided that the importers paid the small duty on the raw substance when it entered the country.

The process of refining opium was sufficiently accepted in Canada for Lady Aberdeen, the wife of 1890s Governor General Lord Aberdeen, to visit an opium factory when she was in Victoria. She was fascinated by the procedure. "Our first visit was to Tai Yuen, an opium refiner. We were shown all the processes from the time it was brought in its raw state, made up into balls the size of the cocoa nut, covered with a mass of dried opium leaves. Then it is split open, put in pans and boiled and stirred and left to cool, and then boiled again." The tarry mass was then packed into brass cans and soldered shut, each can containing about six and a half ounces (184 grams) of opium ready for smoking.

The ritual around smoking was precise: the user took a piece of the processed opium, pulled it and drew it about until it turned a lighter colour. Impaled on a needle, it was dropped into an opium pipe, held above a lamp flame and then inhaled as the drug bubbled in the bowl of the pipe, which was often handsomely decorated and marked with the maker's name. As he (most opium smokers were male) drew in the fumes, he succumbed to his opium dreams. Literature abounds with descriptions of the dens of opium smokers and the gentle haze in which they lived.

In the 1880s, there were about 3,000 Chinese men living in British Columbia, most of them in Victoria. Separated from wives and family, they clung to some traditional habits, among them the smoking of opium. Yet far more opium was processed in Victoria than could be smoked by the city's—or even the country's—opium users. The rapid increase in opium processing was the result of changes in the law in the United States. As in Canada, the attitude to opium in the United States was ambivalent. In an era long before drug prohibition became popular, opium smoking was regarded as something routinely practised by Chinese and nothing to be concerned about. But, said legislators and moralists, it was a hideous trap for white people, especially for any white women caught in the vastly exaggerated "toils" of the opium seller and dragged down to the degenerate level of the opium user.

The American government, however, saw no reason to ban opium use outright, for it did not mind if its Chinese immigrants continued the practice. Instead, the government decided it should be regulated so the government would get its cut. In 1880, in an agreement with China, the United States forbade Chinese citizens from importing opium into the country; henceforth, only Americans would have that privilege. The opium imported at the time was refined by Chinese manufacturers. The United States further declared that only American citizens would be allowed to refine opium—and Chinese immigrants could not by law become American citizens. In addition, a $12 per pound duty was imposed on smoking opium legally imported into the country.

Chinese immigrants in the United States wanted opium and were willing to pay for it. Chinese who were in the business promptly moved north to Canada, most of them to Victoria, and those already in Victoria and New Westminster expanded their businesses. Within a few years, more than a dozen opium factories were at work in Victoria and a few in New Westminster. As Vancouver grew from its founding in 1886, its Chinatown also began to smell of boiling potatoes.

The duty levied on opium imports into Canada in 1881 was just $13,668. By 1887, it had quadrupled; by 1891, at its peak, opium brought $146,760 into government coffers, more than 10 times the amount from just 10 years earlier. The polite fiction existed that the factories were turning out opium for local consumption, but every Chinese person in Victoria would have had to smoke massive quantities day and night to consume what was being produced in Chinatown. Not long after the new American regulations went into effect, refined opium began to move in ever-increasing quantities between British Columbia and the United States.

By modern standards, the profit on smuggling refined opium was slim. Raw opium cost importers about $2.50 a pound, and the Canadian import duty of 25 percent brought the cost up to just over $3 per pound. The city of Victoria collected a licence fee from each opium factory, where Chinese were employed to refine the drug. With the cost of taxes, employees, transport to the United States, bribery of officials and shipments lost to zealous customs officials, thieves or other misfortunes, the cost of the refined opium probably reached somewhere between $7 and $10 a pound. It sold for $12 to $18 a pound to merchants in the United States.

Yet smuggling opium was profitable enough to keep the supply flowing south. Barely a week went by between 1880 and 1909 without newspaper reports about the seizure of smuggled opium. The amount seized and the smugglers charged represented just a small portion of the actual traffic. Thousands of pounds of smoking opium were carried illegally into the United States each year between 1880 and 1910.

Writing in *Harper's New Monthly Magazine* in 1891, Julian Ralph spent considerable verbiage on the smuggling of Chinese across the border. He saved a few words, however, to describe the smuggling of opium, which he suggested was much more profitable than the smuggling of Chinese. Canadians, he said, seemed not at all exercised by the practice because it involved breaking a neighbour's laws and not their own. According to Ralph, it was a moral question, and "the Canadians, instead of taking the bull by the horns, allow the animal to roam unfettered." He wrote:

> There is scarcely a devisable manner of concealment of the little cans in which the opium is put up that is not practised in smuggling this item over our border. It comes in barrels of beer, in women's bustles, in trunks, in satchels, under the loose shirts of sailors, in boatloads by night, in every conceivable way. By collusion with steamboat and steam-shop captains, and through corrupt officials in our own country, the greatest profits are made possible.

The King of Smugglers

Even for the tenor of the times, the words were overblown: Larry Kelly was termed desperate and notorious. Worse for those who believed in strict adherence to the law, he was frequently successful. For 40 years, Kelly, British by birth, Confederate soldier by choice, smuggler by trade, battled the revenuers. Sometimes he won and sometimes he lost, but he never left his calling.

Lawrence Kelly sailed into New Orleans aboard a British navy ship in the early days of the American Civil War. Presumably craving adventure, or perhaps just bored with routine shipboard life, he deserted and joined the Confederate Army. When the war ended, he headed westwards to the Puget Sound area. Some say he swore he'd never earn an honest living under the American flag; certainly, he never tried to.

No one knows when he started smuggling. He was first caught in 1872, bringing Canadian silks across the American border, and was fined $500. That mishap taught him that fines were just the cost of doing business as a smuggler. From that day on, he smuggled anything that promised to make him a profit, from furs to wool to Chinese to opium. Even though he was known as the King of the Smugglers, he was repeatedly arrested and fined or imprisoned, and his cargo confiscated by law officials. But he kept on at the only trade he knew.

Kelly lived in the San Juan Islands with his wife, whom he married when he was 32 and she was 16, putting his property in her name in the hopes it would keep it out of the hands of the law. Barrel-chested, short and broad like a fire plug, he looked rough and tough. His eyes met anyone's gaze. When he was young, he sported a bushy beard, and he grew a floppy moustache when he was older. He had thick, uncombed brown hair that receded as he aged. As a young man, he was also described as wearing a dirty shirt and overalls, his feet bare and browned. A photograph of him when he was in his sixties shows him wearing suspenders and a wrinkled shirt. He had six children. Though he was never known to hurt a child and had no history of violence, his reputation frightened island children so much that, as one resident later noted, "Just the sound of his name . . . made us kids tremble with fear."

Larry Kelly roamed the channels of the San Juan Islands in a fishing sloop until he knew every backwater and every passage. He slipped across the strait to Victoria to load up with illegal Chinese men to be delivered to the United States and then later took on opium, which he could sell at a tidy profit.

We only know about the smuggling trips that failed, the times that he was arrested, which were probably a small fraction of the trips he actually made. Customs agents were well aware of Kelly's activities but generally unable to catch up with his swift boat or even find him as he slipped through the waters he knew so well. Agents suspected that he used Swinomish Slough, near La Conner, Washington, as a place to move opium onto the mainland. Agent Thomas Caine lay in wait for him there on December 21, 1882, but Kelly suspected a trap. He jumped overboard to swim and push his boat ahead of him. When Kelly appeared out of the darkness, Caine boomed out an order for him to surrender. He was caught with 40 cases of Chinese wine and a Chinese man but was fined just $150. The man was apparently an American resident, and the wine wasn't taken too seriously.

By 1886, Kelly had bought property on a small island with a view over Juan de Fuca Strait toward Canadian waters. He loaded opium in Victoria, then slipped across to his home island, where he cached the drug until he deemed conditions right for transfer to his buyers in Seattle or Tacoma. Customs officers were always on the lookout for him. That same year, he was caught in Tacoma with some 300 pounds (136 kilograms) of opium on board, and his boat was confiscated. Yet his fine was a minuscule $100, and he was soon back at work.

Kelly had myriad ways of avoiding detection. He often sewed cans of opium into a sack and towed them along behind his boat, weighting the sack so that it stayed underwater, invisible to pursuers, or tying it to a float when docked, then retrieving it when the customs inspection was complete. Some said that he roped together the Chinese he was smuggling into the United States and tied them to a hunk of pig iron. If chased, he could sling them overboard, and they would sink and never be found. But that story was very probably apocryphal: Kelly said he had never done such a terrible thing, though he had landed Chinese on one side of an island with directions to walk to the other side for pickup, and on occasion, he had landed illegal immigrants back on Vancouver Island, swearing to them that they were in the United States.

"A Smuggler Captured," trumpeted the *New York Times* in March 1891, describing Kelly's apprehension near Tacoma. "Larry Kelly, one of the most desperate and successful smugglers on the coast, was arrested last night on board a train for Portland," the paper reported. Deciding that he was too well known now to run his opium into Portland by boat, Kelly took the train. It was his bad luck that aboard that train was Charles Mulkey, a special agent from the Treasury Department, a man who would later figure in one of the most notorious opium conspiracies in the Pacific Northwest. Spotting the smuggler, Mulkey asked to see what Kelly had in his new satchel. "Clothes," Kelly replied. "Open it up," Mulkey demanded. Inside were 65 cans of opium.

"Larry was mad," the *Times* declared. "He swore that no revenue officer would ever take him, but all the same the arrest was made, and in a few minutes the officers transferred their man . . . to the north-bound train for Tacoma." Mulkey and a police officer hustled Kelly off the train and onto a neighbouring train northbound to Tacoma.

On trial, Kelly said Mulkey had planted the opium on him, but he was found guilty and sentenced to two years at McNeil Island Federal Penitentiary. The authorities weren't through. While Kelly was in jail, they continued their investigation, commandeering his sloop and other property to pay his fines. When he emerged from jail, Kelly seemed to have changed for the worse. He confronted his wife, who was keeping house for another man to support herself, and threatened her with a gun. He frequently appeared drunk.

Suspected of stealing such things as 100 feet (30 metres) of cable, tools and five boxes of codfish to pay the remaining fines, he fled from law officials but was found the next day in a remote location, arrested and handcuffed. He jumped overboard, handcuffs and all, and escaped. A week later, a passerby saw two men at a camp on one of the islands and suspected they might be smugglers. When customs officers arrived, the camp was deserted but some $5,000 worth of opium remained. Was it Kelly's? They weren't sure.

They were sure that Kelly had bought another boat and were pretty sure that he was smuggling again. He was now almost 60 and a little slower on his feet and in his planning. In 1901, he arrived in Seattle from Victoria. He went off for an evening's drinking but imbibed too much and was arrested for drunkenness. The Victoria police tipped off the Seattle police, who searched his room and found two suitcases full of illegal opium. Yet his lucky star still shone: the court fined him an amazingly low five dollars and let him keep the opium.

But Kelly's luck was running out. That same year, he was arrested in Portland and sent to jail for two months for possession of $800 worth of illegal opium. In January 1905, customs inspector Fred Strickling boarded a train near the Canadian border, acting on a tip that Kelly would be on board. Somewhere down the line, Kelly climbed onto the train. Strickling asked to see inside Kelly's valise. Kelly refused, shoved Strickling aside and leapt from the train. Stopping the train, Strickling found 65 tins of opium in Kelly's bags, then had the engineer back the train up. Jumping off, he found his man unconscious and badly cut from his rough landing. He arrested Kelly, and took him to town, but Kelly promptly skipped out on his $1,000 bail.

Larry Kelly was one of the most successful smugglers on the coast, a man who slid in and out of Puget Sound channels with his cargos of illegal Chinese and opium. Customs officer Fred Dean, above, and a fellow officer arrested Kelly for the last time in 1905, on his way from Victoria to Olympia, Washington, with a sloop-load of opium. BC ARCHIVES C-06471

In July, he was arrested again, with a boatload of opium, by customs officials including Fred Dean. This time, he was sentenced to two years in prison. Released early for good behaviour, he was re-arrested for the earlier offence. In 1909, he was sentenced to a further year in jail.

He was 73 years old when he left prison in 1910 and, according to an article in the Atlanta *Constitution*, "broken in spirit and body by confinement . . . his strength is wasted, his nerve is gone and he is without a dollar . . . It is likely the veteran will pass the rest of his days in the poor house and rest in the potters' field."

Despite Kelly's age and failing health, the paper further said he would be followed by customs officials to the day he died. "Measured by the law's standard he is a criminal, but he is whole-souled and generous, ready and willing to divide his last dollar with an unfortunate. He has never implicated others, and he has the reputation of being 'square' with those who profited by his traffic, though he had an opportunity to fleece them whenever he brought a sloop load of contraband goods into the country."

Kelly, said the writer, was a fine mariner and could have made a living on the sea by more reputable means. But smuggling appealed to him as a game of chance, where he could outwit the customs officers by finding a loophole in their "carefully drawn picket lines." Far from being a man of violence, he declared, Kelly had never fired a shot or harmed a single person, a fitting epitaph for the man they called the King of Smugglers.

Kelly found a bed at a Confederate soldiers' home in Louisiana. He died there around 1911.

3

Winning Some Battles, Losing the War

STEALING THROUGH THE WOODS IN the night, four customs agents tracked their prey. Revolvers drawn, they fired again and again, 20 shots in succession. But not a shot hit the fugitive, and he danced away unwounded in the dark, ready to smuggle again another day.

The customs agents were well distant from the West Coast that night in December 1888, staking out their man in Sand Beach, Michigan, on the shores of Lake Huron. But the tentacles of the opium-smuggling octopus were long indeed. The Detroit/Windsor/Sarnia corridor seems to have been a well-used conduit for opium originating in Victoria. In 1887, the *New York Times* suggested:

For some years past, the smuggling of opium from British Columbia to California for the Chinese trade has been a source of immense profit to men engaged in the business . . . The customs officials on the Pacific coast have been making a strong fight against this trade for some time, and about a year ago succeeded in making it so warm for the smugglers that the traffic in that part of the country was practically stopped.

But alas, the trade was soon on again, and the opium was now moved east across the border on small boats or in other ways by middle men, then back west again by train to San Francisco and other coastal points.

The target of the Sand Beach standoff was a Captain Durant. "Everyone around Sarnia knows him to be one of the most daring smugglers who ever exchanged shots with the Customs House officers," reported the *Times*. The story of the non-capture of Durant made the newspapers from Victoria to Brooklyn to Marysville, Kentucky. Durant and two other suspected smugglers reappeared in Sarnia, Ontario, the week after Durant's narrow escape, "all of them . . . young, educated and respected by all who know them," according to the papers. "They are known as the most daring smugglers that ever eluded a revenue officer, and to be agents of a rich syndicate."

Durant and his friend were at their ease in "the swell hotel" of Sarnia and happy to talk with the reporter sent from Chicago to interview them. They had been smuggling opium, wrote the reporter, for two years, often in the capacious pockets of specially sewn coats. Durant wasn't confessing a thing. He had, he claimed, never seen opium, but *if* he were transporting large amounts of it across the border, that was his own personal business.

According to the newspaper story, people in the know were aware that Durant was "one of the trusted agents of a rich syndicate that was organized several years ago for the express purpose of smuggling opium into the United States from the manufactories at Victoria, British Columbia. The syndicate has $5,000,000 behind it, and is largely controlled by C.J. Joslyn of Victoria." Also known as Boss Harris, Joslyn was immensely rich, the reporter claimed, and had told a cashier in a bank that his group had made millions from smuggling opium. He took no risks other than losing money: "He never ventures across the border, for he knows that a big price has been put upon his head."

Did Joslyn/Harris in fact exist? The Victoria *Daily Colonist* repeated a truncated version of the story early in 1889, but made no comment on the man who was said to live in the capital city and was purportedly the shadowy boss of the smuggling ring. He does not show up elsewhere in the annals of opium smuggling out of Victoria. It would be surprising if he were not known in the city where he was said to reside, but perhaps he was successful in keeping out of the public eye.

Other stories indicated that huge quantities of opium

were moving east by rail from Vancouver to St. Thomas, Ontario, then on to Windsor. The boxes were clandestinely moved across the border, then shipped from Detroit by train to San Francisco. Agents of the smuggling ring moved from the West Coast to the east and back again.

Some were less successful at evading official eyes than others. The convoluted case of E.A. Gardner, sometimes misidentified as Irwin Gardner, another miscreant altogether, filled the papers in 1888. Gardner first came to notice as the chief inspector of customs at Port Townsend, where he presumably made the acquaintance of Lady Opium. Together with a man named Chester Terry, he was charged with smuggling 500 pounds (230 kilograms) of opium into the United States aboard the steamer *George Starr*, in a conspiracy with other customs inspectors. He and the other accused, it was alleged, had devised a scheme to switch opium-filled trunks and empty trunks along a route from Victoria to the eastern border of Washington State and back to Portland, then north again to Seattle. Gardner was found not guilty, mainly because the smuggling scheme had been so complex that "the entire absence of opium shown or proven in the case" left ample room for doubt.

Terry, however, was less lucky. Rather than face trial, he skipped out to British Columbia. Despite amassing much money and living in luxury in Victoria, he was reported to have gone insane, and then—or perhaps simultaneously— to have got religion. The great revivalist D.L. Moody came to Victoria in October 1888, and Terry went to listen to him. "He would be the first to enter the hall," at each of the religious meetings, "and the last to leave." He listened with ears and mouth wide open, and "experienced religion in a most ardent form, and it is said his reason has been dethroned." Perhaps it had. His new-found religion caused him to return to the United States to face the smuggling charges, offering land he owned near Tacoma in partial settlement of claims against him.

Even before his trial, Gardner was off to conquer new territory. He was arrested in February 1888 and charged with trying to bring 1,500 pounds (680 kilograms) of opium in a sleigh across the border from Canada to northern New York State. Out on bail, he was rearrested in August on new charges of trying to defraud the government. Once more Gardner was a master of misdirection, and the trail was extremely muddy. He warned police they had better look closely at the "opium" they had found, which turned out to be wooden blocks the size and weight of small opium boxes. "It is plain that the dummies had a double purpose," said the *Times*, first to mislead the government, then to swindle the eventual purchasers. But real opium had been confiscated from the sleigh in the earlier case. Ever eager to confuse the authorities and recover his property, Gardner and his partners stole this opium from the customs lockup.

All the complicated finagling was to no avail. Gardner was found guilty on various charges, including smuggling, and sentenced to a total of 6 years—or 14 according to some accounts—in prison. At least one of his accomplices, a lawyer, turned state's evidence and was not prosecuted.

This Time, We've Really Got It Stopped

We've made a major dent in the opium smuggling trade, crowed the officials of the United States government in 1888 and 1889 and 1901 and almost every year that they arrested and convicted a Gardner or a Terry, or confiscated a cache of opium. With each big drug-shipment seizure and with every arraignment of suspects, they declared another battle won against the opium smugglers. But these victories never added up to an end to the war: a porous border, myriad routes from Canada to the United States and a customs agency vulnerable to bribery and sometimes staffed with incompetents made it impossible to stop smuggling.

The enforcers—customs officials, federal agents and state and civic police—were almost always outgunned and outnumbered. The smugglers used newer and faster boats to fly through the channels between British Columbia and the United States. For many years, the Coast Guard had to depend on the revenue cutter *Oliver Wolcott*, a sturdy but slow ship that could rarely sail faster than four knots. Even Larry Kelly's sloop could move faster than that in a fresh breeze, and *Wolcott* couldn't enter the narrow or shallow waterways used by the smugglers. Most smugglers knew these channels far better than the officials did, and they could choose any time and any place to move through the territory and unload their cargo. The only things the enforcers had going for them were the whispered words of informers and their knowledge of the eventual destination of the opium.

Nonetheless, they tried. Washington Territory governor Watson C. Squire became a US senator once the territory became a state in 1889. Though he shouldn't have been, he was surprised by the extent of opium traffic in his home region. After confessing that customs officials had been unable to stop the traffic in the preceding nine years, he declaimed, "I have repeatedly urged the Treasury Department to take a more vigorous policy in stopping the proceedings . . . The force of the Government employees there does the best it can, but there are not enough of them there."

The best they could do that year was to capture the steamer *Walla Walla* with two barrels put aboard in Victoria, supposedly containing sauerkraut, and on another date with three barrels marked skid grease. Both times, the barrels were found to contain opium when they were opened at the dock at Port Townsend. *Walla Walla* was held under a bond of $5,000, and law enforcers thought they could cause the ship a great deal of trouble, though the ship's officers denied knowledge of the opium—a common defence in those days and these. But it seems they caused *Walla Walla* no trouble at all, for it continued to steam between Victoria and San Francisco for the rest of the year.

A member of the Committee on Immigration of the joint houses of the American government, Squire made recommendations to help stop the smuggling of both opium and Chinese. A bill had been passed authorizing the purchase of two small steam launches that could help the revenue cutters chase down smugglers. "The launches were to cost $5,000 each, to be swift, easily handled, and constantly on duty. They are to play among the islands as police and detective boats. They will be able to do much more effective work than the larger vessels."

Squire recommended that the government add more agents to the West Coast. But, he warned, as long as the duty on opium remained high, "the profits are such that unscrupulous men will take considerable risks. In my opinion, all opium should be prohibited from the country, except for use in the arts or for medicinal purposes. It should be made contraband goods." This would happen two decades later, but Squire would be completely wrong about ending smuggling by making drugs illegal.

A newspaper noted in 1891 that about a ton of opium was stored in the customs house in Port Townsend, "the result of many months' work on the part of the customs officers." The opium, however, was likely to be auctioned off, and if previous auctions were any indication, the smugglers would buy it back for a fraction of its nominal worth, and it would once more be on its way to the eventual user, this time legally.

The US revenue cutter *Wolcott* was overmatched in the battle against smugglers: old and slow, she could neither catch up with the smugglers' boats nor follow them into the narrow passages of the San Juan Islands. Nonetheless, ship and crew did capture a number of smugglers and seize their cargos of illicit opium.
US COAST GUARD

Wolcott and its crew declared a victory in 1891 when they captured five different groups in 15 days, and "the smugglers were all driven to the land for a chance to operate successfully . . . the activity of the *Wolcott* is practically breaking up all smuggling on the straits, which during the last two years has been a perfect harvest to scores of men."

The good work continued. In October of 1891, *Wolcott* captured 13 men on San Juan Island. The Portland *Oregonian* gave credit to the cutter's captain, who had sent one of the steam launches to guard the island the previous week and then dispatched several men to pose as shipwrecked sailors. "They went to the cabin of the smugglers and asked for shelter. After being there for two days, and having secured sufficient evidence against the smugglers, they sent for the cutter." *Wolcott* and its crew apprehended the men and "cut off the escape for the rest." They expected to capture the entire gang, but "the smugglers are said to be well organized and their operations extend over a wide territory."

The new steam launches had arrived in 1891, yet smuggling continued apace. By September 1893, American officials were even more outraged by the practice, and two more revenue cutters were ordered to Puget Sound, one from New York and one from Lake Erie. Both boats were to be armed with rapid-fire batteries of four guns each. The boats duly arrived, but not without criticism: one correspondent to the *New York Times* suggested the assignment was incredibly foolish, for "the unlawful trade referred to is carried on in those waters under cover of night mostly, and in boats, row and sail, through divers bays and inlets, creeks and other shoal waters, where vessels of the revenue cutter service cannot go in chase." It would be far better, he suggested, to break up the "nefarious trade" with more steam launches that could chase down the smugglers' boats.

The cutters did make their laborious way west, but there were problems no ship could solve. Customs officials and police turned out to be eminently bribable, and even a special treasury agent was found to be part of a smuggling ring. Customs and transport officials dismissed for cause, or not, continued to snuggle up to the smugglers, selling information they had gleaned through their jobs. Far from being considered the good guys, efficient agents earned "the bitter hostility of those who have not learned that smuggling is an infraction of the statutes of the United States, and as such is regarded as a crime."

Even diligent and relatively honest officials could not stem the tide of opium smuggling, for a successful operation usually captured only a small fraction of the opium smuggled into the United States. Something more was needed, thundered the *New York Times* in 1903:

> For thirty years, Puget Sound has been the seat of the greatest opium and Chinese smuggling operations in the country, and the Government has spent hundreds of thousands of dollars in attempting to stop small sloops from Victoria or other British Columbia ports . . . They have every opportunity to escape among dozens of islands, and an immense fleet of revenue cutters would be necessary to thoroughly patrol every passage and island coast.

And something more was introduced. The revenue cutter *Grant* was fitted with telegraphic apparatus and could be rapidly dispatched to chase and capture any suspected opium smuggler. The *Times* continued, "Capt. Tozier, who has chased smugglers for years, declared wireless telegraphy will stop smuggling."

But smuggling continued. Six months later, secret agents seized 2,000 pounds (910 kilograms) of opium, worth $30,000. It was the largest amount of opium ever seized in the United States—or so they claimed. They also hauled in one of their Mr. Bigs: "Big" Stevens, along with two other leading smugglers, thus breaking up, they declared, a smuggling ring that had been operating on the sound for more than a year. The catch was credited to a secret agent seconded from New York two months earlier.

And so it went, with special agents, revenue cutters, wireless telegraphy, informers, arrests and confiscations all thrown into the battle against the opium smugglers. But everyone knew the truth: they could reduce the traffic, but as long as demand existed, it could not be stopped.

4

A Convoluted Conspiracy

THE CREW MEMBER ON THE steamship *Haytian Republic* scanned the Columbia River ahead. He saw no sign of the boat he sought and no men waiting on shore. What could he do? The ship was late on its scheduled run to hand over smuggled opium to other members of the gang. After a quick look around to make sure no other eyes were watching, he heaved three barrels overboard and hoped the tide and waves would take them to safety.

They did reach safety of a sort. Two Portuguese fishermen working the river saw the barrels and hooked them out. Now the men who had missed the rendezvous with *Haytian Republic* would have to find the fishermen and make a deal to get their barrels back. Fortunately for the smuggling ring, they tracked down the fishermen, who asked just $5 or $10 for the barrels. But the botched drop-off was a suggestion that things would not go smoothly for these opium-smuggling conspirators.

A comparison of the amount of opium produced in British Columbia and opium actually found by US Customs and the Coast Guard suggests that most opium operations were successful. But there were always exceptions; sometimes smugglers were tripped up by informers or thieves, and sometimes a gang just couldn't get things right. A massive court case in Portland in 1893 revealed that the principals in a long-running smuggling scheme might have been better off in a different business.

In November of that year, American officials arrested 28 men, white and Chinese, and charged them with a long list of offences involving smuggling opium and Chinese across the Canadian border into the United States. The trial revealed the inner workings of a smuggling ring.

Buoyed by their success in smuggling Chinese workers into the United States, Portland businessmen William Dunbar, Nathan Blum and E.P. Thompson decided to extend their operations to smuggling opium. They were perfectly placed to do so. Their company, the Merchant Steamship Company, owned *Haytian Republic* and *Wilmington*, which carried agricultural products and other merchandise back and forth across the border. They had already worked with Major John Wilson, who served as the agent for Merchant in Victoria. Wilson could buy opium from the legitimate Victoria factories, then get it loaded aboard the ships for transport south to Portland and other American ports.

Dunbar and Thompson were respected Portland businessmen; Nathan Blum moved in the Portland underworld of gambling and prostitution. From all accounts, it was Blum who set to work recruiting other members of the ring and bribing customs officials and police in the United States to turn a blind eye to the opium shipments. Their prime catch was C.J. Mulkey, the US Treasury Department agent who had engineered Larry Kelly's downfall. Mulkey was led into temptation by the promise of $1,200 a month, a princely sum for those times, to help out with the smuggling of both Chinese and opium. The ring also recruited James Lotan, Portland collector of customs, who inspected or supervised the inspection of all ships arriving in Portland.

Initially, the smuggling went smoothly. The men devised a simple code whereby Wilson could let the Portland partners know by letter or telegram when shipments would arrive. Their code words referred to legitimate cargo: the words "cheese" and "cement" suggested problems with delivery; itemized lists of wheat, barley and oats indicated various amounts of opium; terms like "soda crackers" and "oyster crackers" indicated how many pounds of opium Wilson should buy in Victoria. "Jelly" was the strongest term: the word commanded a buy of 500 pounds (230 kilograms) of the drug.

In hindsight, the letters and telegrams were barely believable. One letter from Wilson to Dunbar declared that 425 pounds (193 kilograms) of coal had been dispatched from Victoria but had been packed in egg boxes to protect it. The image of coal in egg boxes is indeed laughable.

Once the opium had been loaded aboard ship, the Portland conspirators took over, arranging its unloading, pickup and delivery to the eventual purchasers. But smuggling opium was different from smuggling people. Smuggling Chinese required false documents and a great deal of lying, not concealment of the goods. Opium had to be transported from ship to purchaser. Co-conspirators had to be alerted to opium movements and each member of the gang paid for his involvement. Though the ring made thousands of dollars from its activities, the scheme began to fall apart within the year.

When it did, the law gathered in the conspirators. Dunbar was charged with 9 counts related to smuggling opium; Mulkey faced 18 charges, one of the ships' captains a single charge and another 15 men varying numbers of charges. The grand jury eventually indicted Dunbar, Thompson, Blum and three Chinese on charges of smuggling opium.

When the case came to trial in December, it was reported in great detail by the Portland *Oregonian*. It was marvellous courtroom drama. Prosecutor Dan Murphy, with flourishing moustache, slicked-back hair and wing collar, harangued the jury about the nature of the crime. Many, he thundered, would think smuggling to evade paying duties not a serious crime, but they would be wrong. Duties are used to pay government expenses, "and he who robs the government robs every citizen."

Dunbar's defence attorney, A.F. Sears, was dismissive. The prosecution, he said, had been worked up by "pace-hunting politicians and self-confessed convicts who have been leading lives in violation of the law." Such men, said Sears, were willing to break down Dunbar, a legitimate businessman and good citizen, in order to save themselves "in a most infamous conspiracy to implicate responsible citizens."

Though the report does not indicate it, surely he glared at Nathan Blum. Blum was not in jail but had turned state's evidence, and much of the case rested on his testimony. He calmly agreed that he had been involved in smuggling opium, in partnership with Dunbar, then embarked upon a story that, said the newspaper, "would make an elegant dime novel," frequently looking "smilingly for approval from the court and the audience."

Blum testified that 365 pounds (165 kilograms) of opium had been brought down from Victoria aboard ship on June 4, 1891. The opium sold for close to $4,000. After deducting the purchase price and various other costs, the profit was just over $900, a seemingly small amount for the risks the group was taking.

The money from this shipment was used to buy more opium. Learning little from their first attempt, Dunbar and Blum shipped another 300 pounds (136 kilograms) aboard *Wilmington*. But *Wilmington* was late arriving, and when the opium was once more dumped overboard near Portland, the pickup failed again. This time, the men had to pay a finders' fee of $50 to retrieve one barrel but were lucky enough to come upon the other two on the riverbank.

The October shipment of 500 pounds (230 kilograms) arrived without great mishap, somehow overlooked when the ship was searched by a customs collector, but from then on, the operation turned into a comedy. They hauled the shipment to the house of another conspirator, a Mr. Borg, and repacked it and another 320 pounds (145 kilograms) on hand in playing-card cases. But Mrs. Borg quarrelled with the woman next door, who noted the suspicious activity and reported it to police. Somehow, the conspirators managed to get most of the opium out of the house and delivered to Chinatown merchants before police arrived.

Because deals were not going smoothly, the gang members began fighting with each other. Thefts, seizures or double-crosses now seemed to take place with almost every shipment, and one shipment was seized by customs in San Francisco, acting on a tip from a drayman who had helped to haul the drug, which was packed in playing-card boxes. The informer was duly rewarded with a payment of $840.

Dunbar denied involvement. He could not deny that

opium had been smuggled on board Merchant Steamship Company ships, but he knew nothing of it before the fact. Twenty-nine witnesses took the stand to testify to Dunbar's upright character or Blum's less stellar one, including the mayor and the bank manager, an ex-president of the chamber of commerce, a former Attorney General of the United States, capitalists and merchants, an infantry commander and a former police chief. Asked if Blum would lie, witnesses said yes without hesitation, but Blum just sat tight, "smiling coolly at the witnesses."

Dunbar said he had contacted police as soon as he discovered that opium was being smuggled aboard his ships; he had never bought a single pound of the drug himself, nor did he ever see a hiding place on any of his ships. He had accepted Blum and Thompson as partners in the shipping company because he was facing bankruptcy if he hadn't.

The summing up was more of the same. The prosecution agreed that Blum and other witnesses were of bad character, but they had testified to the details of specific times and places and must not be ignored simply because they were not upright men. The defence then "exhausted the vocabulary of opprobrious epithets in his search for synonyms to apply to Blum."

Blum would, said the lawyer, undoubtedly get a presidential pardon for any crime he had committed, and it was for this that he had turned shamefully on the man who had befriended and helped him. Dunbar, on the other hand, was so busy trying to run his legitimate business that he unwittingly allowed these miscreants to run a filthy business under its cover. Why would Dunbar smuggle? He had everything to lose. The charges were a plot masterminded by the "great United States government," Democrat against Republican, with the sole aim of ruining the defendant.

Not so, said prosecutor Murphy. Blum was just a humble agent helping the government stamp out this heinous crime of smuggling on the Pacific coast. "Never in the speaker's professional experience had he heard such epithets applied as to witnesses in this case . . . Instead of attempting to defend their client, [the defence] had devoted their argument to vituperative abuse of the prosecuting witnesses."

The prosecution carried the day. Just 90 minutes after they retired, the jury returned a guilty verdict on 6 of the 14 charges against Dunbar. He was fined and sentenced to a year in jail. Mulkey was also found guilty of a number of charges and sentenced to a year in jail and a $5,000 fine. Others in the gang were sentenced or fined on various convictions. The American justice system, though, could not touch Wilson, snug in Victoria, and many minor figures in the case, including most of the Chinese, were never tried. Dunbar appealed his convictions, but they were upheld. The gang that couldn't get it right was no more. Worse, two weeks after the smuggling trial ended, most of the accused, plus others, were back in court on charges related to smuggling Chinese into the United States.

CHAPTER

5

The Evil Persists

IN 1907, WILLIAM LYON MACKENZIE KING was shocked to discover the depredations caused by the unfettered use of opium. "Among the well wishers of mankind there can be, I think," he wrote to the Anti-Opium League headquartered in Vancouver, "but one opinion as to the attitude which should be assumed toward this evil which . . . does so much to destroy not only the lives of individuals, but the manhood of a nation."

The following year, King entered government and later became prime minister of Canada. In 1907, though, he was a civil servant, charged with investigating losses sustained during anti-Asian rioting in Vancouver that year. Several of the claims for losses came from opium manufacturers in Vancouver's Chinatown, and King soon discovered what coastal residents had long known about the opium trade. In the cities of Vancouver, Victoria and New Westminster, at least seven opium-refining factories, with gross receipts of between $600,000 and $650,000, churned out smoking opium, most of which was smuggled into the United States.

Even the fraction consumed in Canada, King said in his report, "would appall the ordinary citizen, who is inclined to believe that the habit is confined to the Chinese, and by them indulged in only to a limited extent." To the contrary, he declared, almost as much opium was being sold to whites as to Chinese, and "the habit of opium smoking was making headway, not only among white men and boys, but also among women and girls."

King had visited the opium dens and was appalled by what he saw. He quoted an article in a local paper, which declaimed that "in the beauty and brightness of early sunshine, there emerged into the light, ugly and horrible evidence of the dire influence which the opium traffic is exercising among the ranks of British Columbia womanhood." One pretty young white woman had been found in an opium den; another, no longer pretty, wore "a terrible record of the effects of the indulgence of opium . . . upon her appearance." The only solution, said King, was that the consumption and import of opium should be banned.

He was not alone in his assessment. In China, Australia, Britain, Japan, India and the Philippines, governments were banning opium or calling for a ban. In 1908, Canada made it an offence to import, manufacture, possess or sell opium. Three years later, parliament legislated heavy penalties for anyone found guilty of opium offences and extended the ban to morphine and cocaine.

In 1909, the first international conference to discuss drug problems took place in Shanghai. Front and centre were the problems caused by the opium trade. The conference served as a catalyst for more bans on importing and using opium around the world. That same year, the United States passed the Opium Exclusion Act, forbidding the importation and smoking of opium. The new laws changed the world for smugglers. Smuggling opium was no longer just a thumbing of the nose at customs authorities in an attempt, usually successful, to avoid paying duties. Now it had become a criminal act.

Yet opium smuggling did not stop. Over the previous 20 years, legal importation of smoking opium into the United States had skyrocketed. Though no official figures exist to show how much illegal opium entered the country, it would be conservative to suggest that more than 100,000 Americans smoked the "heavenly drug." Many were unwilling to give up their habit.

When opium became illegal, its price rose steadily as supply dwindled, and many non-Chinese smokers turned to other drugs, such as cocaine, morphine or heroin. Chinese smokers, though, preferred their opium habit, with its rituals and communality. As enforcement increased and penalties became more severe, smugglers turned to ever-more complex ways of moving opium.

One ship's captain told of becoming an unwitting smuggler when crew members brought chests aboard. Unaware, the captain proceeded to San Francisco, but though the customs authorities, alerted by informers, searched from bow to stern, no opium was discovered. Somehow the chests had disappeared. The captain said he had been told by customs officials that some smugglers used cans, similar to condensed milk cans, containing a spool wound with fine twine and a chemical inside. The twine was fastened to a rope, and the can thrown overboard at a drop-off point. Down it went to the bottom of the sea, but when water came into contact with the chemical, it produced a gas that sent the can bobbing back to the surface, where it was collected by the smugglers' confederates.

But the situation had changed radically. Now smugglers needed not only to get the drug into the United States from Canada, but also to get it into Canada to begin with.

Throughout the First World War, opium supplies in both countries were severely limited, but the trade resumed after the war. Organized-crime historian Stephen Schneider suggests that during much of the 1920s, smuggling of opium into Canada remained a small business, undertaken by independents, many of whom brought the drug into the country aboard passenger steamers from Asia or Europe. The federal

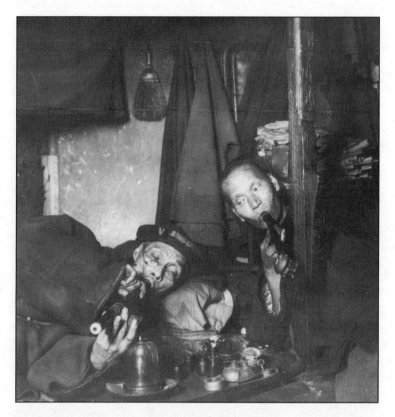

Demand for smoking opium was high along the US west coast in the late 19th and early 20th century. These smokers were photographed in an opium den, probably in San Francisco.
LIBRARY OF CONGRESS LC-USZ62-106914

department of health concluded in 1922, "Most of these illicit shipments are smuggled in by the crews on the incoming steamships, the drugs being carefully concealed below decks, either among the cargo or in the coal bunkers, etc.

Quite a large proportion of such shipments are brought into the country by freight or cargo vessels."

Over time, opium smuggling became part of a larger framework of importing and trafficking in the newer drugs of choice. As the older Chinese died out, smoking opium almost disappeared from the Canadian drug scene. But the smuggling of other types of opium and of other illicit drugs increased; the money to be made was just too big a temptation.

By 1922, according to Canada's federal government, the traffic was "controlled almost altogether by large drug rings, which employ numerous agents to distribute the drug." Much opium passed through Vancouver, some remaining in the country but much moving on. The RCMP reported in 1922 that some 7,125 pounds (3,232 kilograms) of opium entered the port of Vancouver in one year, with 4,500 pounds (2,041 kilograms) being sent on to the United States.

The *Vancouver Daily World* reported on January 16, 1922, that many drugs arrived on passenger ships:

Innocent passengers may be sleeping on it on the way across for a wily Oriental has a knack of hiding it in staterooms under the berths. It has even been stitched into the mattresses. Planks have been pried from the walls and thousands of dollars of cocaine and morphine concealed in cunningly contrived cavities. It has been concealed among the stores on life-boats; in the engine-room store; in the crews' quarters; down in ventilators. It is anywhere and everywhere. Cunningly built up lumps of coal, seemingly innocent enough from the outside, have been broken open and reveal a few thousand dollars worth of dope securely done up in watertight packets. Solid looking blocks of wood have on very close investigation revealed themselves as hollowed out hiding places, the joints so well made and blending with the grain of the wood that only an expert could detect them.

The drugs were then carried ashore by crew members, or in luggage or cargo. Alternatively, they might be thrown overboard and picked up by accomplices.

In previous years, smugglers tended to be white, with Chinese suppliers and Chinese users. After the First World War, some Chinese in Canada took on all aspects of the smuggling business. Chinese crew members hid the opium aboard ship and delivered to Chinese traffickers on shore. Chinese on shore bribed inspectors and gang-plank guards to look the other way and paid the fines for any who were caught. They then sold the smuggled drugs in Vancouver or shipped them inland. But Chinese Canadians were far from alone in the business of smuggling drugs. Stephen Schneider quotes an RCMP report that names the captain of *Empress of Japan* as the head of a gang of drug smugglers that also included crew members. The secretary of the Victoria longshoremen's union was also accused of smuggling drugs ashore.

In 1923, the RCMP took down Frank Eccles, one of their own special agents, and another drug-squad member on charges of collecting smuggled opium from one of the *Empress* ships. Eccles, testified a female witness, had taken her on board *Empress of Russia*, where she picked up 11 packages and concealed them in a skirt that had been specially made to evade detection. Although the packages were so heavy that she almost could not make it home on the streetcar, somehow she managed, and the drugs were picked up by a Chinese courier.

Although at least one of their own members was implicated in smuggling, the RCMP continued to amass evidence. In 1927, they arrested Lim Gim, a wealthy businessman and Chinese community leader in Vancouver. "He has long been regarded as the centre of the opium smuggling traffic in British Columbia," noted the RCMP, presenting their case after years of undercover work. Lim Gim was convicted and sentenced to seven years in prison, but he apparently was able to run his smuggling operations while jailed, and his accomplices still picked up opium from the *Empress* ships. Schneider describes what happened when one shipment came in:

> Around midnight, the informant and an undercover customs officer approached the *Empress of France* in a small boat. They were told to look for a porthole that was covered in a red cloth. After spotting the cloth, the informant attached to the end of a string hanging from the porthole a

half piece of paper that had been given to him . . . The paper
was hauled up into the porthole where it perfectly matched
its other half.

Some 44 tins of opium were lowered to the boat and
delivered to another conspirator at the Hotel Vancouver.
There, and in another hotel room, police found coded documents with details of opium smuggling, together with a
map that showed pickup points for the drug.

Breaking the codes presented a difficult task. The RCMP
brought in Elizebeth Friedman from Washington, DC, one
of the best code-breakers in the business. She deciphered
the code and came to Vancouver to testify in the trial, helping to convict the accused.

But neither taxes, prohibition nor punishment could
end the drug traffic in and out of British Columbia. As the
country headed into the Depression, the Second World War
and the postwar world, the province would become one of
the world's premier bases for the smuggling of drugs.

CHAPTER

People over the Border

IN 1890, ACE INVESTIGATIVE REPORTER Julian Ralph was in the middle of a distinguished career that would take him to China, India, Greece, Africa, every part of the United States and half of Canada, reporting on wars and rebellions, pleasures and pastimes. That year, he made an investigative trip to the northwest United States, attempting to determine the answer to a question that had inflamed the sensationalist press of the region. Were thousands of Chinese being smuggled into the United States from Canada, and if they were, did such smuggling pose a huge threat to the country?

Coming from New York, where he worked for *Harper's* magazine, Ralph was surprised at how much of an issue the purported smuggling was. It had its roots in the Chinese

Exclusion Act of 1882, which forbade Chinese labourers and any Chinese employed in mining from entering the United States, though those who were already there could leave and come back, and Chinese merchants and professionals were permitted to immigrate. Two years later, amendments to the act made it more difficult to leave and return. Further changes in 1888 made it illegal.

The acts were a response to the extreme hostility of many in the western United States to Chinese immigration. Organized white labour hated the Chinese, because Chinese men worked far cheaper and much harder than white men, but their hostility could not diminish the demand for cheap Chinese labour. Nor could it change the desire of Chinese men to enter the United States, where they thought they could earn enough money to return to China after a number of years and make good lives for themselves and their families. Ironically, the prohibition on Chinese immigration resulted in a shortage of Chinese labourers and raised the wages for those who were already in the United States.

Many western Canadians felt a similar hostility, but Canada approached the problem by enforcing a head tax of $50—raised to $100 in 1900 and $500 in 1903—on all Chinese entering Canada. If the person who had paid the tax left the country, he could re-enter provided he had a certificate attesting to his previous residence in Canada.

Though it was discriminatory, $50 was not a particularly high price to pay for entry into North America. Once in Canada, Chinese who wanted to go to the United States could be smuggled south across the border. Ralph was one of many who wrote about the trade. In 1885, for example, the *New York Times* reported on the issue: "The inhabitants of [Puget] Sound ports claim that new Chinamen are arriving every day, and that they were forced to some action to keep themselves from being seriously injured by them. The smuggling of Chinese from British ports to Washington Territory is a very profitable business."

The reporter found himself faced by a conundrum. Yes, certainly the Chinese were willing to work for less, and yes, certainly, if they were not on the coast, then pay for such occupations as wood chopping, salmon canning and other hard labour would have to be higher.

> For there is a particular dislike among laborers on this coast to working for small money . . . The population of the West is an extremely independent one. Every man feels that he can somehow make a living, and if one's prices or the kind of work does not happen to suit, he remarks, with the air of an Eastern millionaire, that "he does not have to assent to the job," and walks away . . . They also get restless and are constantly being convinced that they can do better in some other place than in the one they are in.

The opposition to Chinese labour was strongest among this class of men, for without the Chinese, the picky labourer would claim "extravagant wages." Trying to support white labour, one man hired a white man to chop his wood; that labourer promptly hired a gang of Chinese, paid them half the wages and pocketed the rest.

Thousands of Chinese workers were employed in building the CPR line across Canada; that job completed, many looked south for work. "The temptation to go into smuggling Chinamen across the border is very strong," reported the *New York Times*, "as for each one landed the owners of the boat receive generally $25, a sum which well repays those who make the venture if they escape with their lives, elude the American customs officers, and manage to return to Victoria to claim the money from the agents."

Until 1882, Chinese merchants in Canada and the United States often arranged transport and immigration for Chinese labourers legally entering the United States. Once the restriction act came into force, the merchants continued to be prime movers in smuggling Chinese across the border. Usually, though, the men who took the illegal entrants into the United States were white, for it was far simpler for white men to enter the country without being noticed than it was for Chinese.

The arrival of smuggled Chinese and the presence of legal Chinese in the United States aroused much anger. In 1885 and 1886, labour and political leaders encouraged and led riots against Chinese in Seattle and Tacoma, burning, beating and blowing up property as they surged through the cities' Chinatowns. Attacks followed in smaller towns wherever Chinese workers lived. Troops were called out to quell the rioting but could not stem the anti-Chinese sentiment. When many Chinese in Washington fled to Oregon, further, though less severe attacks took place in Portland. In California, anti-Chinese riots dated back to 1871; expulsions, arson, beatings and even killings occurred throughout the state in the 1880s.

During that decade, newspapers continued to print claims of high profits from smuggling Chinese across the border. A Victoria newspaper article, reprinted across Canada and into the United States, claimed that a three-person Seattle firm had cleared $5,000 for smuggling Chinese in 1884 and explained how it was done:

> The primary move consists in having the Chinamen, or as many contrabands as there chance to be in a party, photographed in Victoria. The photos are forwarded to Seattle, and there exhibited to those familiar with the scheme who are ready, for a consideration, to swear that the Chinaman whose photograph accompanies the affidavit was formerly a resident of the Territory, and left prior to the passage of the Restriction Act.

The affidavit and photo were then forwarded to a Victoria lawyer, who presented them to a customs agent. "If he feels satisfied that the evidence is sufficient, he passes John; if insufficient, he rejects him."

And then there was the switch. Sometimes an American

of good character identified the photo as one of a Chinese man he knew to have been resident in Seattle or some other American place, but who was not there at the time. Then a photo of a different applicant would be substituted for the verified photo, and the affidavit would be accepted.

After the law was changed in 1888, smuggling by stealth became the more common way of getting Chinese into the United States. Though many crossed successfully, some were less lucky. In December 1884, two boats were reported missing. One three-ton sloop with 19 Chinese men and two white men on board was said to have been swamped, with all hands lost. And a leaky boat that left Foul Bay in Victoria in late October with 12 Chinese aboard, bound for Washington Territory, was never heard from again. A third boat, a small schooner, was found bottom up off Dungeness on Puget Sound with the bodies of three Chinese men on board.

Some stories were true; some probably were not. In 1885, a Portland newspaper reported, dubiously, that an Italian boatman had left Victoria with seven Chinese on board. He was intercepted by an American customs cutter. As the cutter approached, he called the Chinese out on deck, struck each man on the head as he emerged from the cabin, then pitched them overboard.

More certain is the story of 24 Chinese men who were aboard a schooner that left Victoria for Puget Sound. For some unknown reason, they were dumped on a rock in

Juan de Fuca Strait. They were discovered and ordered back to British Columbia. The province refused to take them unless they paid the head tax, an amount no one was willing to proffer. The Chinese men were sent to jail in the United States but eventually were taken back to British Columbia and unloaded there.

Frustrating, though not fatal, was the occasional scam played upon the would-be immigrants. In 1901, the *Colonist* reported a story that the reporter cheerfully concluded might be false. An unidentified young white man agreed to take nine Chinese to the United States from Victoria, dropping them on one of the San Juan Islands, from where, he assured them, they could make their own way to the mainland. The cost of $25 a head would be paid, according to the agreement, once the young man returned to Chinatown with a receipt from the "boss man" of the nine.

The group left by sloop in darkness; the next morning, the man returned to Chinatown with the receipt and duly collected his $225. He was not seen again. The following afternoon, "nine weary and bedraggled Chinese walked into Chinatown," and created quite a fuss when they learned the man had been paid for their transport. Shortly after they had left aboard the sloop, a fog had come in. The man had landed them in a place he assured them was the United States and duly got his required receipt. "When the sloop pushed out to sea again they went up to explore. In time they came upon a Chinese place and soon discovered they had been outwitted. Then they walked back." They had been landed, not in the San Juans, but on the shores of Sooke, on Vancouver Island.

More gruesome is an oft-repeated story about smuggler Ben Ure, who lived on an island in Deception Pass. There is no doubt that Ure smuggled Chinese into Washington aboard his small boat. It is said that Ure's wife would signal him as he approached the pass, to let him know if it was safe to proceed. Some claim that Ure tied the Chinese in burlap bags; if danger threatened, he would throw them overboard to drown, and the currents would take the bodies to what became known as Dead Man's Bay.

It was to sort out truth from fiction that Julian Ralph arrived in 1890 to write his *Harper's* article. Were the Canadians worried by reports of people smuggling? Not so you would notice. "They come here to enter your country," one influential Canadian told Ralph, "and you can't stop it, and we don't care."

Ralph was indeed amused, or bemused, that the only time Canadian authorities did something about smuggling was when the steamer *North Star*, "after a busy career in violating the laws of our country without interference by Canadians, had at last excited their displeasure by returning from our border with smuggled goods upon which the Canadians impose an import tax." The owners of the ship were charged with failing to provide bills of lading for their cargo, failing to answer all questions with regard to cargo and crew, and failing to take out proper clearance papers and to produce any smuggled goods.

Ralph noted that the steamship line that brought tea, rice, opium, oil and Chinese immigrants to Canada profited greatly from the money paid in passages, making at least $200,000 over three years. The Canadian government profited from the $50 per person head tax. And the two-way traffic benefited some Americans as well, for the ships could smuggle back into Canada such things as playing cards, gambling layouts and whisky.

Following twisted lines of communication, Ralph decided that the smuggling of Chinese across the border was a business "of small extent and petty results." Between 1887 and mid-1890, some 4,000 Chinese men entered British Columbia. He believed that at least half of those men were smuggled into the United States.

He confirmed that many of the Chinese entering Canada were committing fraud as well, writing that, "Chinamen who go away from Canada looking at least forty years of age, return appearing to be only twenty-four; and others who measure five feet and nine inches when they depart, come back in a few months several inches shorter or taller." Many went to great lengths to look like the man who had left. Ralph noted, "One of these tricksters arrived with a great scar burned in his forehead, a cut disfiguring one cheek and a deep pit burned in his neck." All to no avail: the man under questioning confessed he had never been in Canada before.

Ralph was highly critical of American policy that refused re-entry to Chinese labourers who had come legitimately to the United States but were refused re-entry once they left. It was, he said, "unconstitutional, Unchristian and dishonorable" and an affront to victimized men, many of whom had worked long and hard to build the western United States.

Opium and People, People and Opium

As Julian Ralph noted, the smuggling of Chinese south across the border often went hand in hand with the smuggling of opium. If you had connections in the Chinese community in Victoria, where you bought opium to take into the United States, you might well use those same connections to smuggle Chinese labourers across the border.

The long and convoluted 1893 trial in Portland that saw Nathan Blum testify against William Dunbar and other conspirators accused of smuggling opium was followed that same year by a trial of 28 men, among them Dunbar and customs agent Mulkey, as well as half a dozen Chinese merchants from Portland, on charges of conspiracy to smuggle Chinese into the United States.

The trial revealed an intricate smuggling network. According to testimony, Major John Wilson approached Chinese merchants in Victoria to obtain lists of Chinese who might want to enter the United States illegally. The merchants provided the names and sent the Chinese men to Wilson and the steamship line. A price was paid for the landing of all illegal entrants, and men such as Portland collector of customs James Lotan and treasury agent Mulkey made sure that they were allowed into the United States. Nathan Blum and other witnesses for the prosecution described the acquisition of forged birth certificates, residence certificates and other identity papers that illegal immigrants carried with them so that the bribed American officials could claim that their entry was indeed legal. But there were many hitches in the business, including certificates that were wrongly filled out, missing photographs and claims that moneys had not been paid.

The case against the accused turned largely on Nathan Blum's testimony. Claims and counterclaims ricocheted around the courtroom as spectators crowded in to hear what the Portland *Oregonian* termed "the great smuggling case . . . the case of the century."

The judge summed up very carefully. For lack of sufficient evidence, he directed the jury to acquit a number of the defendants, including a ship's captain, several other accused conspirators and all the Chinese accused, except for Seid Back—a merchant who frequently acted as an interpreter when the ships arrived in Portland—and Ching Ghong Quie. There was not a great deal of evidence against Quie, he said, so the jury must decide whether enough had been said to convict him.

But in the cases of six of the defendants, including Dunbar, Mulkey, Lotan and Back, the judge suggested much more consideration was required. There was no doubt that Chinese had been illegally landed; the jury must decide about the guilt or innocence of the accused. Given such a large hint, the jury took just a day to review the mountains of evidence and decide that Dunbar, Back, Mulkey, Lotan and the two others were guilty. Nathan Blum was duly rewarded for turning state's evidence. Although others remained in jail during the trial, he was put up at a hotel and left as soon as the trial was over for Washington to seek a pardon for himself and another conspirator who had testified in the trial. The *Oregonian* wryly reported:

> As they have not yet been sentenced, it would seem they are rushing things; but probably they would like to be pardoned before they are sentenced, as they might then claim that they were not convicted of an infamous crime . . . If they are pardoned perhaps the infamy will be removed from them, and they will go on the stand [in trials yet to come] purged and purified and with good reputations—of the kind.

With that, the *Oregonian* closed their books on the trial, which they termed "the greatest legal event of the age [that] has no parallel in this history of this section." Appeals in the case went all the way to the Supreme Court, but the original verdicts were upheld, and Dunbar, among others, went to jail.

The great smuggling ring was no more, but there were many more individuals and groups still eager to take on the profitable smuggling of Chinese into the United States.

7

Cowboys, Liars
and Lawmen

THEY CALLED HIM COWBOY, and perhaps that was the right nickname for Jake Terry, for he was the epitome of recklessness and derring-do. From 1873, when he shot a saloon owner over a disputed bar bill and was sentenced to five years in jail, to the day he died at the hands of a vengeful husband, shooting and lying were his specialties. And so was smuggling: Jake Terry was one of many independent smugglers of people, drugs and other goods who worked outside the more organized groups of conspirators.

Jake Terry was just 20, newly arrived in Washington State from Missouri, when he was sentenced to a jail term for the saloon assault. Once released, he got work on the railways. He quickly recognized that the railway route from Mission, British Columbia, to Sumas in Washington State was a smuggler's dream.

But lawmen might be watching the route for smugglers, unless they could be persuaded to look the other way. Though proof is scarce, it is probable that Terry bribed customs official Zachary Holden and King County deputy marshal George Poor. The story that follows varies according to the teller, but there is no doubt that one man died, one was wounded and Terry ended up back in jail.

Terry probably paid Holden and Poor to help him smuggle 15 Chinese men across the border. The two officials went to Skagit County, where they met newly appointed customs inspector J.C. Baird. Alerted by the two to the possible smuggling of Chinese, Baird told them to cover one road while he and his deputy James Buchanan covered another. Terry went north with Holden and Poor.

But Baird and Buchanan had their own suspicions. Unknown to the trio, they made for the railway tracks where the three others were headed. At about 10 PM on July 26, 1891, while concealed beside the tracks, they saw three white men leading a dozen Chinese up the tracks. Baird ordered the men to stop. Buchanan later said in court:

> We were just going to capture the Chinamen . . . When the shooting commenced we were twenty or thirty feet from them . . . The white man in the lead shot first . . . It was

necessary for me to shoot to preserve myself. I could have run but I would rather have it in my face than in my back . . . Yes, I fired to kill.

And kill they did. Poor cried out, "I'm shot! I'm a deputy!" and fell dead on the ground. Terry was hit four times but fled the scene with the third white man, presumably Holden. Baird found Holden in a hotel in a nearby town. Terry was also tracked down and charged with smuggling.

Back in town, with no proof of who was lying and who was telling the truth, the authorities arrested everyone, including Baird and his assistant. Terry pleaded guilty to smuggling and was sentenced to 10 months in a penitentiary, plus another 30 days because he could not pay the fine assessed. Baird and Buchanan were convicted of manslaughter in Poor's death but released because it was concluded that they had acted in good faith. Doubt lingered, however, and Baird and Holden were asked to resign from the customs service. It seemed the only winners in the case were the smuggled Chinese; during the melee, they melted into the bushes when the shooting started and were never seen again.

Terry was not deterred by his imprisonment and Poor's death. As soon as he got out, he started smuggling again, moving Chinese and possibly opium south across the land border throughout 1893. He was no luckier—or no more skilful—this time; caught once more, he was returned to jail.

When he was released, he went back to breaking the law, this time counterfeiting 10-cent coins, not exactly a high-profit business. Off he went to jail again, convicted as a career criminal and sentenced to 10 years at hard labour. This time, he was dispatched to San Quentin, a much tougher prison than the state penitentiary he had become accustomed to.

Repentance and reform were alien to Terry. He was probably a member of the gang that helped infamous Canadian outlaw Bill Miner rob the train at Mission Junction in 1904. But the law had no proof and could not touch either man. Terry went home to Washington State, where he told the Seattle newspaper that he'd had nothing to do with the robbery but knew who had done it.

Terry said he would only talk to the railway men directly if he was paid to do so, but it didn't happen, for most believed that he had been part of the train robbery. He moved on to Port Townsend, where he started smuggling again, dividing his time among Chinese, opium and other goods. But he was restless and wandered back to Sumas for Christmas of 1905, where his ex-wife Annie still lived. "Ex" meant nothing to him: Annie had remarried, but he threw her new husband out of the house twice. Two days later, the husband and a posse of his pals strode up to the house to take back what was legally his. Terry fired and followed them as they fled down the street, shooting over their heads. His shooting spree continued for a week, though he hit nothing and no one.

Terry was arrested, but Annie bailed him out, and he skipped north to Canada, where he began smuggling again, this time concentrating on moving opium south across the border. Too foolish or too arrogant to stay in Canada for long, he walked back into Sumas and into the house where Annie and her husband lived. The husband ordered him to leave. Terry refused, so the husband shot and killed him.

All Sumas was delighted, for they well remembered Terry's shooting rampage of the previous year. Many Sumas residents chipped in to pay the husband's bail; he never served time for the killing. Annie left town.

The Bellingham newspaper, *Daily Reveille,* summed it up:

> Terry during his lifetime was the hero of many an inspiration for a dime novel writer. According to his own statements and one of them which is borne out by the records of the state penitentiary, he has done almost everything which any bandit might be supposed to do in order to be real up-to-date. He has robbed trains, after sticking them up, smuggled opium and Chinamen, and been an all-around bad man for years aside from being a partner in crime with the notorious Bill Miner who is now serving a term for train robbery in Canada.

Who Knew that Smugglers Lied?

It was a matter of honour, or dishonour, and the talk of Seattle, Port Townsend and Victoria in 1897. Were letters incriminating prominent Chinese and white citizens forged or genuine? If genuine, they were dynamite. The letters purported to come from Port Townsend customs interpreter Yee Gee, supposedly sent to a co-conspirator, Ng Hok Hank, and had been found by Hok Taw, who was known in Victoria for being on the wrong side of the law.

The scheme was one of wheels within wheels. A man identified as the "Rev." J.E. Gardner, a prominent American member of Hok Taw's group, declared that Hok Taw had found six letters on the dock at Victoria and had sent them on to Gardner, who turned them over to the law in Seattle. If truly written by Yee Gee, they deeply implicated Puget Sound customs collector James C. Saunders in a scheme to smuggle Chinese from British Columbia into the United States.

The main letter read in part, "Our company has contracted to land thirty people from China per each boat, and there have been eighteen trips altogether." In Chinese, the letters said that $500 for the current shipment should be given to Yee Gee's nephew. And the conspirators did not have to worry about being caught, for Saunders was in on the scheme.

The letters, duly translated from Chinese, were produced at a preliminary hearing charging Yee Gee with being involved in smuggling Chinese. They suggested a conspiracy among the Chinese figures in the case and Saunders, and that Saunders wanted to be paid immediately the money he had been promised for helping the smuggling ring. The case produced some hysteria across the nation, as newspapers such as the Albany, New York, *Evening Journal* screamed that 1,000 Chinese had been landed through Port Townsend as a result of the big conspiracy.

Had Yee Gee in fact written the letters? Never wrote them, never saw them, he told the court, raising enough doubt that he was not committed for trial. But if he had not written them, who had? Shortly thereafter, Hok Taw was arraigned in court in Victoria, charged with forging the letters. Charges and countercharges flew around the court-room, as witnesses testified that the letters were or were not in Hok Taw's hand and that the print of the personalized good-luck seal, or "chop," was that of Yee Gee or of Hok Taw. It was not a simple matter for the judge to decide, since both Chinese and the question of chops were alien to him.

The reporter for the Victoria *Colonist* had a fine time describing the testimony of the various witnesses. The accused sat "smiling placidly," while a witness had a "mild countenance [that] beamed behind a pair of gold-rimmed spectacles." As the trial progressed, Yee Gee got angrier: he insisted that warrants be served on a special agent of the US Treasury, whom he said was implicated in the false accusations against him, and the shadowy pseudo-reverend J.E. Gardner, who also worked as an interpreter, saying they had robbed him of various papers and seals. That case seems to have been dropped after the two were arrested. Yee Gee himself was charged with trying to bribe Gardner, but that charge also disappeared.

On the day before Christmas, doubtless shaking his head, the Victoria judge set Hok Taw free despite strong evidence that he had written the incriminating letters. The judge remarked "upon the difficulty of sifting Chinese evidence . . . The court intimated that it seemed as if both the prisoner and others had engaged in smuggling Chinese and the present trouble had grown out of the fact that there was too much competition in the business to please both."

It could be, too, that Hok Taw had good reason to want Saunders out of the way. Two years earlier, the *New York Times* had commented on Saunders' energetic work: "Collector Saunders began a pursuit of Chinese and opium smugglers so relentless as to call down upon him the denunciations of a previously supposed disinterested class of people." In the process, Saunders discovered that "a very large proportion of the people living along the shores of Puget Sound [hold] the smuggling of Chinese and opium across the Canadian frontier to be a worthy business."

After the breakup of the opium and Chinese-smuggling ring that involved treasury agent Mulkey, and the arrival of the energetic Saunders, the price, said the *Times*, for moving Chinese across the line increased from $10 a head to $80. "Smuggling under the new Saunders regime became so risky that the revenues of the Puget Sound district sufficiently advanced to make the district second only in importance on the Pacific coast to the San Francisco district." Everyone on the smuggling side was incensed at Saunders. If he truly could not be bribed or induced to relax his vigilance, it was small wonder that smugglers might try to have him removed by other means.

Throughout the 1890s, enterprising smugglers continued to move Chinese by land and sea into the United States. Four sloops containing Chinese were seized near Port Townsend in one six-week period in 1890; one had arms on board and an extra set of sails, buff in colour, less visible than white sails. Other ships set their course for California. The schooner *Halcyon*, for example, left Victoria in the fall of 1892, reportedly with Chinese and opium aboard, then reappeared six weeks later with neither cargo. A crew member reported she had stopped in California.

Smuggling was always a good story, and a *Colonist* reporter interviewed "an interested sailor man" in 1892. The sailor described himself as the kind of patriot who "hustles John Chinaman out of the country in the hold of a 15-knot steamer, after safely securing all the money they have about them, to circulate in British Columbia."

The reporter continued, "He said the [ship] *Iona* had 45 passengers at $65 a head; that they had clearance papers for 'Frisco, and would have made it sure if they hadn't 'broken down.' The Chinamen understand their business, and, when ordered to pack, lie down, straight out, like herrings." The Chinese smuggling business, the reporter stated, had reached gigantic proportions. A steamer out of Vancouver had been losing money for five years; she loaded aboard a cargo of Chinese at English Bay, landed them in the United States, hopped over to the Hawaiian Islands for a "cargo of dope," loaded and then took it into the United States, and the owners were in funds once more, the profit for the voyage being $15,000.

Into the 20th Century

He was clever, he was wily, he was picturesque. Everyone knew that James Kelly smuggled Chinese men, opium and anything else that would turn a profit from Victoria to points on Puget Sound; he was considered one of the four most successful smugglers in the region. "His pretensions, with attempts to lead an honest life, were the scantiest semblance towards labor," declared his obituary in the Victoria *Colonist*.

Yet he was caught by the forces of law and order only once. In 1900, Kelly pointed his small boat, with six Chinese aboard, to Kanaka Bay on San Juan Island. But a US revenue cutter was on his trail and trapped him in the bay. There were no gunshots or protests. Kelly smilingly agreed that he was guilty and paid the price, a year in prison. However, "Officials familiar with the character of the man attribute no benefit from the imprisonment," the *Colonist* continued. He cut back after 1900, but made one last surge, displaying "an energy that had brought about the belief that he had resumed his former criminal operations. Without visible means of support, he appeared with large sums of money and an unusual show of prosperity." Kelly died in 1908, putting an end to a thriving and lucrative career.

At the start of the 20th century, career smugglers like Kelly and opportunists who saw possible profit still smuggled people across the border from British Columbia to Washington and coastal points to the south. A steady drop in references in newspaper articles, however, suggests that either the number of people smugglers was dropping or that the smugglers were getting better at evading the law.

The decline of smuggling probably had much to do with the increasing weapons deployed against operators such as Kelly, as the American government poured more money into suppressing the trade in people and drugs. In 1904, the revenue cutter *Grant* became the first ship on the west coast to be equipped with wireless telegraphy. The *New York Times* heralded the installation of the equipment as a fine way to stop the smuggling of Chinese into the United States. The *Times* pointed out that the advantages the smugglers had would be somewhat counteracted by *Grant's* wireless operations. If the ship's crew caught sight of a suspicious small boat skirting the shore, they could immediately send a wire to customs officers in Port Townsend or Friday Harbor, who could speed out in fast launches to intercept the unsuspecting smuggler.

Would the new technology work over the mountains and through the forests of the country around Puget Sound?

Record-breaking masts of some 220 feet (66 metres) were erected, and the officers in charge were extremely pleased with the result.

The government also turned its attention to smuggling by land. In 1903, the United States opened a new detention station for Chinese on the border at Sumas. The CPR, which operated the rail line south to Sumas, agreed that it would deliver all Chinese riding its trains directly to this station. Anyone found to be illegal would be immediately deported back to China. To help them out with the difficulties of false identifications, the immigration service employed the Bertillon biometrics system, a way of measuring a person so that he could, according to the proponents of the system, be clearly identified as a certain individual. Immigration officials would also be seeking changes to the law, so that the burden of proof of previous residence or membership in the merchant class would fall upon the Chinese seeking entry, not the American government.

A smaller amount of smuggling also took place farther inland. In 1906, a US Customs official and two Chinese men were charged with smuggling Chinese and opium across the border from British Columbia into Montana. At Rossland, Chinese workers looked south for jobs as mining declined in the West Kootenay town. The Rossland *Miner* suggested that the town was the "favorite rendezvous for the pig-tailed hordes that swarmed across the international boundary on their way to big cities in the States," and spoke of "the frequency with which strange Chinese are arriving in Spokane." The "hordes" were, however, probably quite minimal.

Other changes in the first decade of the 20th century affected the smuggling of Chinese. When the head tax for entering Canada climbed to $500 per person in 1903, the incentive to evade the tax grew as well. In 1907, newspapers reported what seemed to be a well-organized conspiracy to smuggle Chinese into Canada through Vancouver. Officials noted that each night several Chinese were hovering around the CPR ship *Tartar* in rowboats. They kept watch and then searched the ship by light of day. They discovered 13 Chinese stowaways: 3 in the forward part of the ship and 10 in the coal bunkers. "When found, the stowaways were grimy with coal dust," the *Colonist* reported, "and, needless to say, hungry, though none showed signs of extreme suffering from their long confinement." Evidently, Chinese crew members had fed and helped them during the voyage.

All 13 were deported on the next-departing steamer. That same month, a Hong Kong man, T.C. Hopkins, was fined $500 and sentenced to three months in jail for helping a Chinese man get illegal passage on *Empress of India*, bound for Victoria. The stowaway was found and charged with illegal entry. "On the voyage, he mixed with the other passengers, but on nearing port he was put in a chest in the quarters of the master at arms [the prime mover in the smuggling case] and was in the chest for three days."

As in that case, crew members were almost always part of the conspiracy to smuggle Chinese ashore in Canada or the United States. In 1910, the chief officer of the liner *Oceano* was found complicit in smuggling three Chinese into Tacoma. The liner had, it appeared, dropped off 17 men in Vancouver, then proceeded to Tacoma with the remaining three still aboard, hidden in the ship's coal supplies. "Had it not been for a yell made by one of the number in agony when he was prodded by a large iron rod with which the customs men were drilling in the coal, seeking for hidden opium, the Chinese would not have been discovered." The accused crew member, E. Loftus, was "well known in Victoria, where he has a number of friends." The charges were dismissed because there was no concrete evidence linking Loftus to the stowaways.

With the passage of the Chinese Immigration Act in 1923, completely banning further Chinese immigration into Canada, smuggling became more difficult and less frequent. It would not end, however, as long as there were Chinese who desperately wanted to enter the United States or Canada and men who were willing—for a price—to help them do so.

8

From Japan to Canada

THE CAPTAIN OF *SUIAN MARU* was content. Holding a glass of beer in his hand, he smiled as he looked around the high-class geisha house. How very nice of people who had chartered his ship to take him and his senior crew out the evening before they sailed. And, yes, a little more beer would be much appreciated.

The next day, hungover and exhausted, he was not so happy. After a glorious night at the geisha house, his hosts had poured him and his crew members aboard the boat. Then the ship had put out to sea with, thought the captain, some 50 men aboard for a fishing trip out in the islands far north of Japan.

Then the trap was sprung. While the captain had been

imbibing, cronies of the hosts had brought aboard another 30 people, three of them women, and hidden them below decks. Now, out of sight of land, the gang leader explained the new plans to the captain. The fishing schooner was not going fishing. They were going to Canada. No one would ever believe, they said, that the captain had not been involved from the beginning in this conspiracy. He had no choice but to go along.

Chinese were not the only nationality to arrive illegally in Canada early in the 20th century. The first Japanese immigrant into British Columbia, Manzo Nagano, smuggled himself into Canada as a stowaway in 1877, but by 1900 the number of Japanese in British Columbia was still fewer than 5,000, almost all of them legal immigrants. Then, in 1906, *Suian Maru* sifted in through the darkness in the first known large-scale attempt to land Japanese immigrants illegally in British Columbia.

At night, *Suian Maru* hove to along the coast just northwest of Victoria and lowered her boats. Seventy-eight men clambered down from the deck and were rowed to shore. Under cover of darkness, the group moved from the beach to the nearby forest. At first light, they formed up into columns and began their quixotic quest to march the 30 miles (50 kilometres) or so from their landing place to the head of the Saanich Peninsula, near Sidney. There, they had been promised, a steamer would pick them up and take them across the strait and up the Fraser River, where they would work off the debt for their passage at a cannery and saltery co-owned by Oikawa Jinsaburo, who had arranged for the trip.

It must have been a strange sight. Many of the men had just emerged from the Japanese army and the Russo-Japanese War of 1905 and still wore some or all of their army uniforms. Off they marched in military fashion, "pockets bulging with army biscuits . . . with meat and condiments," reported the Victoria *Colonist*. "The party was supplied with shelter, tents, hammocks and maps." These important and detailed maps, in Japanese, showed them a route that avoided any main roads and marked the location of the Japanese section of Victoria and houses that were occupied by Japanese. Anyone who could not keep up with the column was left behind to make his own way to whatever destination he could find. Just 26 men arrived in Sidney. No steamer awaited them, but the police did.

After *Suian Maru* had dropped off most of the men, it was spotted by authorities "hovering about Beecher Bay in a suspicious manner." Trapped by light winds, the schooner was still there when the quarantine officer reached the area later that day. We've been fishing, the captain told the authorities and pointed to the fishing lines on deck as evidence of their activities, but the lines were clearly new and had never been used. The captain said that the weather had been so bad at their fishing destination in Bering Strait that they had run south and east, heading to

New Westminster to buy salt salmon instead. Challenged again, the captain admitted they had landed a number of Japanese illegals on the shore. But perhaps there was a way out of this small difficulty. "Without attracting attention he slipped a little packet of gold coins into the pocket of [the quarantine officer]. The doctor felt the jingling store of gold, and put it aside as an exhibit in the case." The captain, however, was confident that his attempted bribe had been successful.

The mate, too, tried to put over the false story. "The mate was suave," reported the newspaper. "He held to his tale until the evidence began to accumulate. Finally, he looked over to the captain and he said, 'Skigaiaganai,' which means, in effect, 'It can't be helped.'" The mate and captain then admitted the ship had sailed across the Pacific with the sole purpose of landing the illegals on British Columbia soil.

The newspaper was somewhat perplexed by the whole attempt. At that time, Canada placed no restrictions on Japanese immigration. In order to leave Japan, an emigrant needed a passport and permission to leave; in order to enter Canada, he needed to pass a medical examination. The reporter conjectured that those on board the schooner had failed to get exit permission or feared they would not pass the health examination.

Escorted into Victoria, the captain was very unhappy. According to the *Colonist*:

[He] is a very serious man. He is not only worrying with the fear of prospective imprisonment for his share in the expedition, though it is generally stated by the Japanese that he started from Oginohawa with the belief that he commanded a fishing expedition, but he is worrying too for fear that he will lose his expected decoration for service on Japanese transport during the recent war. Imprisonment will mean the cancellation of any award made on this account.

Eventually, all the passengers were captured. The captain and the ship were charged with landing the group at a place other than a port of entry and without passenger lists or permission. Fines were levied against both. The story disappears from the newspapers, though the reporter predicted the fines would be paid; if they weren't, the ship would be confiscated and the captain imprisoned. The captain presumably returned to Japan, his hope of wartime decorations still alive.

All of the passengers were permitted to stay in Canada. They still owed Oikawa for their passage and went to work for him on two islands at the mouth of the Fraser. Though Oikawa—for whom one of the islands is named—returned to Japan in 1917, most of the immigrants stayed in Canada, and some of them and their children were sent to internment camps in 1942. A plaque in Richmond commemorates their voyage.

It was not Oikawa's first attempt to bring Japanese into the country to work for him. He had brought in Japanese immigrants legally but paid them so poorly that they rebelled and refused to continue working. A second attempt, this time to bring in Japanese illegally, was stopped by Japanese authorities. Oikawa was sentenced to jail, although the sentence was subsequently reversed. The voyage of *Suian Maru* was his third attempt, a voyage so celebrated that it became the subject of a novel written in Japan.

One of the men who helped negotiate to keep the *Suian Maru* immigrants in Canada was Fred Yoshy, a clerk at the Japanese consulate in Vancouver. Writer James D. Cameron notes that this was just the beginning for Yoshy, who went on to help smuggle many more Japanese into the country. When the Canadian government, faced with climbing immigration from China and Japan and frightened by an anti-Asian riot, imposed controls on Japanese immigration in 1907, Yoshy saw not limitation but opportunity.

By this time, Yoshy was the interpreter for the immigration branch in Vancouver, and he had much scope for illegal activities. From the end of the First World War through to the 1930s, he took advantage of his post by convincing his superiors he should examine would-be immigrants by himself. He then allowed various illegal immigrants to stay in the country—for a price. Though suspicions repeatedly gathered over his head, his superiors, either in on the plot or happily ignorant and somewhat lazy, continued to deny that there was anything wrong going on.

In 1928, an informer told the RCMP:

> Yoshy and his partner . . . are trafficking in smuggling some innocent Japanese into this country by way of using naturalization certificates. The partner in Japan trains Japanese applicants to some extent to fit them to be examined at a Port of Entry in Canada for precaution's sake, but it is so arranged that this Fred Yoshy is always to meet these immigrants at Vancouver, because this Yoshy is allowed to examine these Japanese immigrates by himself alone.

By 1931, it was impossible to ignore Yoshy's involvement in human smuggling. The RCMP collected fraudulent birth certificates, naturalization certificates and statements about Yoshy's activities. He was arrested, but witnesses in the case disappeared, possibly fearing that they would be deported, or worse, if they told the truth. The charges became a cause célèbre, reports ricocheting through newspapers across the country. Later that year, Yoshy was finally convicted of conspiracy and of unlawfully receiving a gift while employed by the government and was sentenced to two years and six months at hard labour in the BC Penitentiary. It is thought that he returned in Japan in disgrace after he served his jail term.

9

Anything At All: Smuggling Lite

THE SUN HAD BARELY RISEN when the customs officer began his rounds along the Oak Bay waterfront in Victoria. Something aroused his suspicions, and he hastened along the beach. There in the sand close by the water lay two incubators. Just offshore, a schooner, all sails flying, was headed out "at a steamboat rate" toward Discovery Island.

"Aha," thought the officer, "what have we here? Someone has clearly been smuggling." Doubling his suspicions, a horse-drawn wagon came rumbling down the road to the beach "giving him a new idea as to the mysterious proceedings going on around him." It was too late for him to hide and watch what went on, so he hailed the two men in the wagon, one Chinese, one white. They denied that they were doing anything wrong and trundled back away from the beach.

Too late, the customs officer decided he should have stopped the wagon from leaving and found out who the men were. "There was," recounted the *Colonist,* "good reason why such an outfit should be secured." The large white sailing vessel was believed to have come from Bellingham Bay, presumably with the two large incubators aboard. "They are of immense size, and were evidently intended for someone entering the ranching industry," possibly to be used for hatching chicks.

The officer believed that the schooner had landed far more than just the incubators, but there was no sign of any other contraband. The incubators were seized for evidence, but presumably the trial never took place, for there is no further mention of the case in the press.

Such was the lighter side of smuggling in 19th- and early 20th-century British Columbia. There was very little that could not be smuggled into or out of Canada if there was enough profit in it. In 1907, for example, a "vigilant customs officer" spied a Chinese woman coming off a ship much stouter than when she had begun her visit. A subsequent search after she tried to run away revealed a large parcel of embroidery from Hong Kong. In 1908, three "Italians" were caught as they made their way off the ocean liner *Empress of India.* They had, they said, gone aboard to see about getting a job, but they carried a bundle with them when they left.

Opened by customs, it revealed embroidered shawls and other goods.

Sometimes the courts decided that accused smugglers had not been smuggling at all, according to the letter of the law. In March 1897, eagle-eyed customs officers searched the cargo aboard the steamer *Walla Walla*. Destined for San Francisco, the ship listed bales of sheepskins, salt hides and similar cargo. But "information received, of an unusually reliable character" suggested not all was so innocent. "Cunningly concealed within them [the sheepskins] were deer hides of no small value." At the time, the export of raw deer skins was illegal. A subsequent trial revealed that 777 skins were hidden on the ship.

However, said the first judge, there was no evidence that an illegal act had been committed, since mere possession of the skins was not illegal. Yes, said the second judge in the appeal court, but according to the Customs Act, the onus was on the accused to prove his innocence. The case must be retried. In January of 1898, the accused smuggler was again acquitted. "May I have my deer skins back?" he asked. No, said the Crown, we want to appeal again. By then, though, the papers seemed to have tired of the case, for nothing more was reported.

The hue and cry over the exportation of deer skins was far from over. The following year, dealers tried to send off 50 sacks of "raw hides" on *Walla Walla*, treated in such a way that it was difficult to ascertain what kind of animal they came from. Again, authorities accused them of smuggling illegal raw skins. The would-be exporters claimed the export was perfectly legal because the skins had been partially tanned. To prove their point, they had a witness clean and dry a hide in court. The defence submitted correspondence with the government agreeing that tanned hides were legal for export. The prosecution brought forward a learned witness from the provincial museum who said the skins were not tanned.

In the end, the court found for the defence, and the charge of illegal export was dismissed. The company, which had found an American market for deer hides, was now presumably able to ship the 18,000 it had on hand, in addition to the 3,000 already shipped. Legislators were poor losers. In the next session of the house, a member proposed new wording for the Game Protection Act, trying to prevent the indiscriminate slaughter of deer. The argument about the export of skins went on for years, some saying that to allow the killing of deer and the exportation of skins, raw or not, would practically exterminate the deer population on Vancouver Island—a somewhat ironic prediction given today's reality.

Finally, in 1904, the legislature passed an act making it illegal to kill a deer in order to sell any part of it and banning the export of any deer hide, whether raw or tanned. It is not known whether this ended the trade in skins or if smugglers simply became more adept.

Some smugglers took advantage of the long land border between British Columbia and the United States. The *New York Times* carried a squib in 1900 alluding to "a great deal of smuggling in recent days." Miners' supplies were once more in question, but this time the smuggled goods were headed south. Two men had attempted to lead five pack horses loaded with goods from British Columbia to the mines in the Mount Baker district of Washington State, but were caught near the border.

In 1905, another customs inspector told of all the smuggling that went on between rural areas of the Fraser Valley and towns across the border to the south. Many farmers, he said, saw no harm in crossing over to buy the supplies, machinery and provisions they wanted. "They have no intention of smuggling . . . it is simply a matter of convenience and saving of time. Reports have circulated that livestock and immense quantities of groceries have been brought across without the knowledge of customs."

That same year, readers were all agog at the idea that "about a thousand women of Vancouver, Victoria and other cities are wearing dainty apparel on which the duty has not been paid," a duty that would have amounted to about 35 cents per item. The smuggler in this case did himself in. As he was selling the "waists," he saw a Turkish boy whom he accused of defrauding him of $60. At the police station, the boy turned on his accuser, and the story of the shirtwaists emerged. His method of smuggling was to "place about 100 waists in two overcoats, roll them up on a seat or in the racks and cross the line, which he always did without difficulty."

As opium smugglers had discovered and liquor smugglers during American Prohibition would gleefully determine, the inlets, straits and island coastlines just across Juan de Fuca Strait from Vancouver and Victoria were an open invitation to smuggling. So frequent were the dashes from one side of the border to the other with foodstuffs, supplies, machinery, liquor, cigarettes and farm produce that few outside the customs services of the United States and Canada gave the trade a second thought. Every once in a while, though, customs officers would swoop. In 1887, for example, the *New York Times* reported that the ship *Ida Wilson* had been seized by Canadian customs officers, who took possession of 300 sheep and other stock on board. "It is said," reported the *Times* with remarkable straight-facedness, "that smuggling has been systematically practised in this locality."

In 1894, a customs officer, possibly the same one who had come upon the incubators, "happened to be out at Oak Bay" one evening when he saw a small American boat landing something. He made an inventory of the groceries thus landed and then seized them and the boat, much to the captain's disgust, since he had no other way of getting home. "Investigation into the sloop's smuggling operations brought to light the fact that she was bringing the goods at wholesale from the American side, to be retailed in this city."

Cigars and tobacco were other popular items with smugglers and their customers. A ship's pilot from Seattle was arrested in 1898 and charged with smuggling cigars from Seattle to Victoria. He had, authorities suggested, been doing this for some time, and various small hotels around town were offering the smuggled items for sale. In 1908, "what the inland revenue officer believe to be an organized scheme of smuggling was nipped in the bud last night, when they discovered in the bar of the Negro Porter's Club, on Water street, a box of cigars without the necessary label." They were very good cigars too, 20 cents each if brought over legally. The secretary of the club was fined $50 and costs.

What fun it was for the reporter: "This is a tale," revealed the *Colonist* in 1908, "of daring-do on the waterfront; of the bold, bad contrabandist and the exciseman; and of how the customs man played detective and a cigar dealer and a captain paid a fine of $100 for smuggling some tobacco."

The exciseman had apparently done work worthy of Sherlock Holmes, much in vogue in 1908, finding three caddies of smuggled tobacco that had been delivered when "the lynx-eyed customs man" was not there to see it. Though the customs agent had his suspicions, he could find nothing when he searched. He waited and saw an expressman drive away from the address he was watching and go to a schooner on the waterfront. He pounced and discovered the contraband on board, resulting in arrests, trials and small fines all around.

The following year, customs seized 3,300 cigars at Nanaimo from the ship *Georgia*. Finding them had not been easy; a preliminary search turned up nothing, since they were hidden in the water tank. Believing himself safe, the Chinese smuggler took the cigars out and prepared to sell them, but he was turned in by a shipmate.

Chinese wine, tobacco, cattle, sugar shipped south in sacks, apples, shoes and playing cards were all opportunities for the smuggler—as were strawberries. In 1894, customs officers captured a 25-foot (7.5-metre) sloop at Cadboro Bay and confiscated its load of "the best strawberries Orcas Island can produce, which were being smuggled for sale here."

The best sting of all took place in an attempt to stop wool smuggling. Through to the 20th century, wool was cheaper on the Gulf Islands and Vancouver Island than it was on the San Juans and in Washington State. A hefty tariff was imposed on any wool brought south; records showed that almost no wool had been legally imported over the years, although much wool had been sold. But short of actually catching the smugglers in the act of crossing the border and landing fleeces, how could illicit wool be identified?

In a 1902 dispatch from the American side, a reporter outlined the situation. Many Native people, he wrote, were raising sheep along the east coast of Vancouver Island, especially on the Saanich Peninsula, and on the small islets on the Canadian side of the border. Stuart Island, "long bearing an ill name as a smugglers' rendezvous, is said to be the centre of operations on the American side."

In the dark of night, the Native sheep farmers arrived on the rocky shores of the American islands with bales of wool. Met on the beach by the crews of small, fast sloops, they turned over the wool in return for whisky, tobacco, calico cloth and guns. According to the reporter:

> Very quietly, the sloops are loaded with the white bales. Without lights they slip away into the blackness, while the natives noisily make their way back to the large potlatch houses . . . Once away from the shore, the sloops with all sail on, make speedy passage to the American side. The run of a few miles is soon accomplished. The wool is stored in the warehouses. Unlike stamped opium, it cannot be identified. With that of his own flocks, the smuggler can market it openly and without fear.

In 1905, customs agents came up with an answer to the problem. In sheep-shearing season, two agents disguised themselves as seal hunters and rowed a small boat across to the Canadian islands, where they began visiting every sheep ranch they could find. How interesting this process is, they said to the ranchers, meanwhile inserting surreptitiously into the fleeces wooden skewers that could not be seen from the outside of the bale.

Customs had long been sure that Alfred Burke, a resident of the San Juans' Shaw Island, was a frequent smuggler of many items, wool foremost among them. On South Pender Island, the disguised customs agents came upon Burke, described as small, of quiet demeanour, some 70 years old, "bent and wrinkled and gray, but still active, agile and alert," according to the Seattle *Post Intelligencer*. Burke was travelling in a slender rowboat stained dull black so it could not easily be seen from a distance. They had a chat, then watched as Burke set out for Orcas Island. The agents followed; in a store warehouse, they found half a ton of wool, run through with their skewers. They arrested Burke, but he evaded charges because the customs officers had not actually seen him cross the border with the wool. The wool was confiscated and sold, depriving Burke of his anticipated profit.

The customs officer in charge was confident they had seriously reduced the amount of smuggling that would henceforth take place. "[He] is determined to make wool smuggling so hazardous that few are likely to engage in it," the *Post Intelligencer* declared.

By 1907, customs agents boasted that large-scale smuggling on Puget Sound had been stopped for good. "We have been unable to unearth anything exciting for a long time." They still had to watch for a few Chinese or Japanese who tried to smuggle themselves south, and Canadian fishermen occasionally would try to send their fish to the

American side. They found a little opium on board boats, but "as far as the smuggling operations go our experiences with operators are decidedly limited in number these days," reported a lieutenant aboard a US revenue cutter stationed at Port Townsend. "They are not operating on a scale of any size and in my estimation have deserted the water as their field of action and try now to get across the border by train or in teams."

Little more than a decade later, when the United States banned the sale of alcoholic beverages, the situation changed completely.

10

Not a Drop Shall Pass Their Lips—But It Did

AMERICA DRANK ITS CHRISTMAS TOASTS and celebrated New Year's Eve, 1920, with its usual exuberance. Two weeks later, on January 16, 1920, the United States went dry.

Even before 1920, two-thirds of the states had enacted their own prohibition laws, but a determined man could always cross a border and find a place to drink legally. Then, propelled by the Women's Christian Temperance Union and the Anti-Saloon League, politicians all across the United States voted to ban the manufacture and sale of any beverage that contained more than 0.5 percent alcohol. The Volstead Act then defined and put into practice the 18th amendment to the US constitution.

Opponents of alcohol greeted the legislation with joy.

The day Prohibition came into effect, barnstorming evangelist Billy Sunday, who preached to huge crowds in tent meetings across America, declared to 10,000 people at a meeting in Virginia, "The reign of tears is over. The slums will soon be only a memory. We will turn our prisons into factories and our jails into storehouses and corncribs. Men will walk upright now, women will smile, and children will laugh. Hell will be forever for rent."

At least that was the theory. In practice, it worked the way moral prohibitions usually work. Americans were not about to be denied their whisky and rum, bourbon and beer. Some turned to distilling "bathtub gin" for their own use or for sale. But the greater number wanted the quality and consistency—not to mention the ease—of commercially produced alcoholic beverages; they wanted to be able to go out for a drink or have a few with the boys. Fortunately for them, just to the north and south were countries that permitted the manufacture, sale and export of alcoholic beverages.

Some alcohol was smuggled into the United States from Mexico and the Caribbean. Some came all the way from Europe or from countries in the Pacific. But what better place to procure your supplies than from that reliable and friendly neighbour just across the very long, very undefended and almost completely permeable border? Fleets of small boats put out from Atlantic and Pacific ports, bearing loads of bottles south along the coast. Cars and trucks carried sacks and boxes of the stuff along back roads at night. Cases of booze were hidden under loads of coal or grain on freight trains crossing the border. Every possible conveyance was used: rafts and horses, shank's mare and even airplanes. And because smuggling and selling alcohol were very profitable but involved breaking the law, men were killed, government agents were bribed to turn a blind eye, and smugglers made a fortune, all in the cause of keeping America wet.

The stories of the lawlessness that came with Prohibition are legion. On the West Coast, mobsters and Mafia were less in evidence than they were in Boston or New York; there was no Al Capone or Bugsy Moran, no St. Valentine's Day Massacre. Eliot Ness walked the mean streets of Chicago, not Seattle. But liquor nonetheless flowed south. Prohibition brought the largest epidemic of smuggling ever experienced on the West Coast. Though no one can be sure of the exact total, hundreds of thousands of bottles were smuggled out of British Columbia and into the western United States between 1920 and December 1933, when politicians acknowledged a failed experiment and repealed Prohibition. Even one noted advocate of temperance had to admit that Prohibition had created "an orgy of lawlessness and general corruption."

How It Worked

As was true for opium smuggling, the liquor smuggler usually committed no crime until he crossed the American border. Edmund "Butch" Fahey, who spent a decade smuggling liquor from eastern British Columbia to Spokane, noted the difference. "The Canadian attitude was that Prohibition was both idiotic and an infringement of a free man's rights . . . In the Dominion, he [the smuggler] was looked upon by the gentry as a bonafide businessman engaged in legitimate business. In the States, he was a felon, hunted by officers of the law."

Where the American saw illegality, the Canadian businessman saw opportunity. British Columbia law dictated that wholesale liquor must be bought from a government-approved export house. Not surprisingly, the number of these houses near the border multiplied rapidly once Prohibition was declared. In Victoria and Vancouver, for example, the number increased from 16 legal export houses in 1921 to more than 30 a year later.

The buyer, whether American or Canadian, obtained his liquor from the export house. The journey of the liquor from the point of purchase varied, but much went by sea. Some liquor obtained in Victoria was transported by Canadians running 18-foot (5.5-metre) boats to one of the Gulf Islands that snuggle up to the American border. Boats dispatched from American ports slipped into these harbours, loaded up the liquor and quietly motored back, usually by night, to some point the smugglers considered safe—a hidden bay, perhaps on one of the San Juan Islands—then onward by small boat when the coast was clear to a rendezvous point in Puget Sound or the San Juans.

Some liquor was run down the coast in small boats from

Victoria or Vancouver to the docks in Port Townsend or Seattle, where it was loaded onto trucks and delivered to the eventual user, often under the unseeing eyes of a customs official. Some was taken aboard by ships large and small at Victoria or Vancouver, duly and legally labelled for landing at some Mexican or South American town. Was the boat actually capable of such a long journey? Was it reasonable that large loads of liquor that had arrived in British Columbia via the Panama Canal and the long journey up the Pacific coast would be shipped back down that self-same coast? It didn't matter: as long as the Canadian legalities were observed, no one in Canada was going to stop the process.

As the 1920s wore on, liquor smuggling by sea became bigger and bigger business. The small boats that dashed across the border to land their liquor were often contracted by large Canadian export firms; if the captain or crew were caught, the firm would pay their bail or their fines. Larger ships, known as mother ships, also put to sea, carrying vast amounts of liquor. They sailed south, then hove to out of sight of land, beyond the three-mile (five-kilometre) US territorial limit. Small boats, alerted to their location by messages passed by telegraph, short-wave radio or agents in their city, sped out to the mother ship, loaded up and were away again in a very brief time.

Away from the coast, rum-runners, most of them American, drove across the border, travelling by night on back roads. They loaded up at warehouses in Greenwood,

Fernie and in the Fraser Valley and usually headed back at night, evading border patrols along the way and delivering the booze to their customers.

All these methods demanded some co-operation from US border agents and police. Many a customs agent or border patrolman made extra money by ignoring smuggled liquor; sometimes the corruption reached high into the customs service. Had the smugglers been dealing in drugs or other suspect contraband, bribery might have been more difficult, but many Americans thought liquor smuggling hardly a crime at all.

What motivated the smugglers? For many, especially those higher up the smuggling chain, it was just a business proposition. There was money to be made with minimal risk. But many who made the runs down the coast or across the border by land were entranced as much by romance and risk as by the promise of easy money.

Charles "Cappy" Hudson captained one of the mother ships that ran down the coast to meet with smaller boats dashing out from shore. One-time Royal Navy captain of a Q ship (a heavily armed merchant ship designed to lure submarines into ill-conceived attacks during the First World War), he received the British Distinguished Service Cross and Bar for bravery. Demobbed, he immigrated to Manitoba and tried to run a farm. Four years later, losing money every year, he headed to the West Coast to try to get back on a boat. He was hired on to a "sealer" that turned out to be a rum-runner. He couldn't believe his luck. "After losing money for years on the farm and working like a slave, what a change to receive $400 for about 6 days pleasure," he told a writer in the 1930s.

He was hooked. "We considered ourselves public philanthropists! We supplied good liquor to poor thirsty Americans who were poisoning themselves with rotten moonshine." Described as adventure-loving, flamboyant, gentlemanly and a man of courage and action, he had discovered a trade that gave him all the excitement of war without the risk.

The Big Boys

With eight bedrooms, eight bathrooms, an art deco ballroom panelled in silver leaf and complete with a sprung dance floor, vaulted ceilings, porte cochère and almost 21,000 square feet (1,950 square metres) of living space, Casa Mia in south Vancouver was an astonishing mansion in any age. It was even more remarkable considering it was built at the start of the Depression in 1932. It was the house that smuggled liquor built, its owner one of the West Coast's biggest liquor barons. The Depression was not quite so depressing for George Reifel, or for his brother, Harry, who had his own mansion just up the street. Rumour had it that the Reifel brothers stored liquor to be smuggled south in a tunnel that connected the two houses, but like many another rum-running story, this one was a myth.

The story of Casa Mia was part of the romance of liquor smuggling during Prohibition days, a romance that rides on tales of bullets flying and small boats slicing their way through waves and darkness to bring alcohol to thirsty Americans while evading pursuing government agents. The real foundation of rum-running, though, was business, and a very profitable business at that. Fortunes were made—and rarely lost—by the men who ran export houses in Vancouver and Victoria, Fernie and Greenwood and a dozen locations in between, supplying the runners who took most of the risks.

In 1920, German immigrant and brewmaster Henry Reifel, father of Harry and George, didn't take long to recognize that Prohibition could become a bonanza for Canadian businessmen. By 1926, he and his family owned four large breweries and distilling companies and operated export houses to supply smugglers who carried their product into the United States. Their rival in the business was the Consolidated Exporters Corporation (CEC), formed in 1922 by various brewing and distilling companies. CEC opened a large warehouse in downtown Vancouver, close to the railways, roads and harbour along or through which most of their product would move. There was room for both interests and others besides; in the first six months of 1923 alone, liquor houses in British Columbia sold more than a million dollars' worth of liquor every month.

The American press was fascinated by the size and efficiency of the liquor-running establishment headquartered in Vancouver. In 1923, the *Los Angeles Times* sent a reporter north to find out about the business. He reported back:

> Here in Vancouver, whisky is no outlaw . . . liquor and the liquor traffic is trenchant . . . it is blatant, it laughs at the American law. Down in Coal Harbor, you will find it—the "whiskito" fleet—halibut boats that have forsaken an honest calling—pleasure craft used exclusively as law violators—fast trim boats that can sail circles around the ancient obsolete American patrol boats. In big offices—in dingy warehouses downtown, and along the waterfront you find the other element of liquor and the liquor interests—the keepers of the export houses, the firms whose only reason for existence is the fact that America is dry.

The reporter had no difficulty at all arranging to buy a shipload of liquor. He found a bartender in a Granville Street club who introduced him to the manager of an export warehouse, "a large building practically filled with whisky, wine and champagne, 90 per cent of which will ultimately be delivered into the United States."

As the decade wore on, both the American enforcers of Prohibition and the export houses became more sophisticated. US Customs and the US Coast Guard acquired faster and better boats, hired more agents and kept a watch on those who might be corrupted. They found and paid informers in the trade who were willing to tell what they knew about upcoming runs. In response, the big boys of West Coast smuggling devised better methods of communication, devising codes to be used for telegraph messages between mother ship and shore. The Americans complained about the smugglers' use of wireless telegraphy to evade capture, so the Canadian government pulled the wireless licence of one of the rum-running ships. The company concerned then hired a young amateur shortwave enthusiast—a precursor of today's computer nerds—to devise and run a system of short-wave transmitters for communication between the ships and the main company office. These ham radios were camouflaged and kept out of sight on the ships, in case customs officials came aboard.

Communication became a battle between the deviousness of the export houses and their runners on shore, and the ingenuity of the enforcers. By 1926, the Americans had decided that they needed cryptanalysts to break the smugglers' codes. This task was easy at first, since the companies were employing just two main code systems; however, once the rum-runners realized that their codes were being broken, they devised some 50 different systems, many of them more complex than any used by the government for its own security operations. CEC, for example, hired a returned navy man to devise better and more secure codes.

As she had in the battle against the opium smugglers, Elizabeth Friedman worked at breaking the liquor smugglers' codes. In her US Coast Guard office in Washington, DC, Mrs. Friedman analyzed messages intercepted by the

Coast Guard on the West Coast. She was usually successful, and her transcriptions were sent off by mail or telegraph,
depending on their urgency. In June 1928, she was dispatched
to the coast to train others in decoding messages to which
she had found the keys. Between May 1928 and January 1930,
more than 3,000 messages were logged between the ships on
Rum Row and headquarters in Vancouver. Most were deciphered and many resulted in the Coast Guard intercepting
boats at sea.

David Kahn, the author of a book on code-breaking,
noted that once the smugglers discovered that their codes
were being broken, they diversified. From two codes that
changed every six months, they expanded their cryptogra-
phy to a different system for almost every ship on the coast.
"In May of 1930," he notes, "the Consolidated Exporters
Corporation, with three shore stations, employed a different
cryptosystem from its headquarters to each of its 'blacks,' or
rum running craft, while the mother ship corresponds with
these blacks in an entirely different system."

The highly complex codes were just part of the big-
business reach of the major exporters. Among other
companies, Henry Reifel ran Joseph Kennedy Ltd., linked
with and named for the man who would become the father
of an American president. A Royal Commission struck in
1928 to investigate the liquor business declared that the
only business of this subsidiary was to export liquor to the
United States.

Nothing that the commission uncovered was news to people on the West Coast. In 1926, an undercover police officer wrote to an RCMP official, declaring that "among waterfront employees, such as Stevadores, Checkers, and Police, with whom I conversed, it is the opinion that a large quantity of the trans-shipped liquor [liquor supposedly intended for Mexico or other non-US ports] never reaches the Ports to which it is consigned, but is landed in Canadian waters, and ultimately returns to Vancouver for distribution among local bootleggers." He pointed a finger at such companies as CEC and Reifel's operations. But they were not alone: accusations of bribery and undue influence, some of them well-founded, were hurled at Members of Parliament, police officials and deputy ministers, all the way down to simple customs inspectors.

That same year, a US grand jury indicted 38 people they termed members of a Pacific Coast liquor-smuggling ring, charging them with conspiracy to violate the National Tariff Act. Among the 38 were all the stockholders in CEC. Though the charges may have acted as a deterrent, they resulted in few convictions or penalties.

CHAPTER

11

Liquor by Land

THEY LOADED THE LIQUOR IN fast cars with bumped-up suspension and bulled their way across the border, sometimes fleeing through a hail of gunfire. They hid the booze in barns or cached it in the woods. They concealed the bottles under the back seat and sat the kids on top. They wired logs together and floated loads of booze downriver on the Kootenay or the Columbia; they loaded up horses and pointed them toward home across the border. It wasn't the heavy-duty smuggling of Victoria and Puget Sound or Vancouver and Seattle, but communities just north of the line from the Fraser Valley to Fernie sent liquor to the border towns and cities of Washington, Idaho and Montana. There was money to be made from Prohibition, and the locals had no intention of missing out.

Spokane lies just 112 miles (180 kilometres) south of the British Columbia border and was connected to the province in the Prohibition era by a railroad and a skein of highways and rough back roads. Spokane resident Butch Fahey ran a roadhouse on the outskirts of Spokane. Though serving alcohol was illegal, Fahey had little trouble with lawmen, who were more concerned with catching rum-runners than penalizing rum-servers. Faced with paying an exorbitant price for smuggled liquor, though, he decided to take a shot at the rougher side of the business to get his booze for half the price. Including bribes and other costs, it would cost him $32 to $36 for a case of liquor that he could sell for $70.

For almost a decade, Fahey ran liquor across the border, though his wife frequently beseeched him to get out of the trade. He found it competitive but fair. "Every man hauled for himself and himself only. There was no organized racket running the smuggling in our area. On several occasions a guy tried to move in and be a big shot, but, in true western fashion, his ambitions were always curtailed."

Fahey made his first trip with a one-armed driver through snow and ice on narrow twisting roads, discovering the hard way that car problems were often the nemesis of the rum-runner. Three tires blew out along the way because he had neglected to check whether the car they were using had newfangled heavy-tread tires rather than old ones with thinner treads. From then on, he checked and double-checked the cars he used. A blowout when outrunning the revenuers, a blown gasket or a malfunctioning fuel pump could mean great delay, the loss of a cargo or even the loss of liberty.

Most of Fahey's trips were made at night. He and a driver would head north across the border, buying liquor from the warehouse in Fernie or Greenwood. The next night, they headed south again, crossing the border on rough roads and narrow tracks, always watching out for the Prohibition agents. Once they got the liquor across the border, they often cached it in a barn of a friendly—and well-paid—farmer until it was safe to run it by night into the roadhouse at Spokane.

Fahey and his driver were forever seeking new routes along isolated roads where they could be fairly sure the border patrol and federal agents would never venture. One Canadian back road led them to a railroad trestle over the Kettle River. "To cross it in a car was a hazardous adventure, requiring the utmost alertness on the part of the driver. A single miscalculation with an automobile meant a drop into the churning river far below." But the men at Canadian customs and the railway office were ready to help out. When Fahey arrived, they loaded the liquor onto the handcar they used on the tracks and then very carefully drove the car across the bridge. It was a simple matter to push the loaded handcar to the other side, then unload it into the car and and drive away.

Everyone knew that Fahey was trafficking in smuggled

liquor. On one occasion, police chiefs and sheriffs' officers at a convention in Spokane dropped by the roadhouse for a drink and were offered the hospitality of the house. To be successful, Fahey and his fellow rum-runners needed to pay bribes. Customs officials and Prohibition agents were paid to look the other way or to avoid a certain place at a designated time.

Fahey didn't always run his rum by car. Sometimes he used the railroad through northern Montana, with the liquor hidden under coal. But this was more complex, with more payoffs to more people. Sometimes, even payoffs, luck and skill were not enough. On one run, he arrived at a bridge to discover three border-patrol officials with drawn guns waiting at the far end of the bridge. Knowing a jail term awaited if he stopped, he decided to run the blockade:

> I ducked down in the front seat, holding the steering wheel in a straight line and passed at terrific speed. Bullets tore out my windshield and all the other glass, including the rear view window. I had to raise myself in my seat to make the right angle turn onto the main highway. At the speed I was travelling, and in the short time I had after sitting up straight, I had to have full command of the wheel to negotiate the turn. With the greatest of luck, I made it and came out of the affair without a scratch.

He was convinced the agents had shot to kill since they could readily have disabled the car by shooting out the radiator. Fahey never carried a gun: "When they are shooting at you, sometimes blasting the windshield in front of your face, you might if you had a gun, do something on the spur of the moment that you'd repent your remaining days."

After some eight years in the business, Fahey's luck finally ran out. He was arrested, charged and sentenced to six months in jail and a $2,000 fine—the light punishment the result of brilliant arguments by his lawyer. When he came out, he discovered that the business had changed. Greedy smugglers had boosted the retail price too high, moonshine was becoming more popular than smuggled liquor, and gangs were taking over what running there was. He lamented, "There was no attempt at honesty any more. What had been a runner's private adventure with, usually, no harm to anyone but himself had turned into a dirty racket that soon after financed the wholesale smuggling of narcotics." It was the end, to him, of the golden age of rum-running.

Many others ran liquor across the land border in the first decade of Prohibition. Some reports suggest that even the Doukhobors, the communal religious community around Grand Forks that did not use alcohol, helped out with rum-running. According to one account, a small plane would fly from Spokane to a Doukhobor farm just across the border, where the liquor was cached. The plane would load up at the farm and carry the liquor back to the United States. If the plane was damaged on arrival or simply needed repair before it took back to the air, a First World War veteran and small-plane owner in Spokane would receive a message and fly to the Doukhobor landing strip with spare parts and mechanic's savvy, though he refused to get involved in the actual smuggling.

A railroad ran from Rexford, Montana, to the coalfields near Fernie—a fine route for booze. Some men rode the train to get their own private supply of liquor from the main liquor-supply warehouse in Fernie; others were more enterprising. "One day we were going down to a place they call Four-Mile just out of Fernie," Fernie pioneer Jim Constanza told local historian Gary Montgomery, "and we saw the two cars at the crossing and this train was there and these guys were loading sacks of booze into the coal car."

According to his daughter, Fernie resident Oliver Abbey built flat-bottomed boats for smugglers who would load up on the Canadian side, then ride the Kootenay River south. The first load was lost when the boat hit rocks, but many more successful trips followed. Another local recounted that smugglers loaded a boat with whisky and "turned it loose and met it on the other side of the line. And they'd take wire and tie two logs together and load the whiskey on and let them go. They bootlegged every which way you could imagine." One man bought a plane to run booze; others loaded liquor into Indian wagons, topped it with tents and then sent the wagons across the line via an obscure route. Studebakers, Hudson cars and Model T Fords could all be modified to take loads of liquor south. Of course, if the smugglers were caught, their cars were confiscated. The police chief or another agent would get the car or it was sold at auction.

Fernie resident Tyler Lindberg described the trade out of Fernie to Montgomery. "The road down to the States was just a ditch. They'd get stuck, bust a drive shaft, bust an axle, my father'd take the horses out. They'd unload the whiskey and nobody'd know a thing about it . . . The cops were comin' around all the time; they didn't know where it went." Sometimes the smugglers would hide on one side of a curve and wait for the Prohibition agents; when the agents' car appeared, they would jump out and push it over the bank.

The end of Prohibition in 1933 was preceded by major enforcement initiatives by the "dry agents." In 1932, smugglers were pushed west by energetic pursuit. They were no safer in Montana. Historian Gary Wilson recounts that customs officers stopped one smuggling convoy of eight men—four Montanans and four Canadians—in eight cars, with 4,000 quarts (3,800 litres) of scotch, bourbon, rye and beer coming south from Canadian points.

On the north side of the border, reports of gunfire were rare indeed. But violence occurred in one celebrated case because rum-runners were transporting liquor across a provincial border. In 1918, Alberta outlawed the importation of liquor, while British Columbia still made its export legal. Emilio Picariello, a Fernie and Alberta businessman, was not impressed; he had been sending liquor into Alberta from Fernie for several years, and he had no intention of letting the law stop him. He ran liquor across the provincial border despite all attempts of the Alberta Provincial Police (APP) to stop him. Occasionally, they'd catch a car loaded with sacks of liquor, but often the cars got through.

In September of 1922, the APP got word that Picariello was coming through. The police stopped him when he crossed the border, so he honked to warn his son, Steve, that there was trouble and then blocked the road with his car so Steve could hustle back to British Columbia. Constable Steve Lawson tried to stop Steve Picariello, firing in the air and then at the car, slightly wounding the smuggler. But Lawson's car got a flat tire, and the younger Picariello was able to retreat back to British Columbia.

Emilio Picariello also headed home. On his way, he and Lawson and other APP members confronted each other, with taunts and threats shouted from both sides. When Picariello learned his son had been shot—though he did not know how seriously he was wounded—he went back to challenge Lawson, taking with him Florence Lassandro, a young woman who was married to a confederate. The two men soon came to blows, and either Picariello or Lassandro, depending on which version you believe, shot and killed Lawson.

Picariello and Lassandro were arrested, tried and convicted. Although there was considerable doubt as to Lassandro's role, both were hanged. Lassandro was the last woman to be hanged in Canada.

12

Two Kings, a (Hi)Jack and Working Rum Row

JOHNNY SCHNARR WAS OFF Cape Flattery when the engine of the small boat he was steering began to act up. Johnny was an ace mechanic and worked out the problem, filing and sandpapering the valve stem until the engine ran smoothly again. But he had a bigger problem: on his first trip on the rolling waves of the open ocean, he was seasick. A huge southeaster didn't make him feel any better, and he was dismayed to discover that the boat would run out of oil and gas long before they completed the projected 10-day trip to San Francisco. They'd have to put into port.

Not a good idea, said Harry, the boat's owner, since they were carrying a contraband supply of smuggled liquor and the bar at the mouth of the Columbia was a huge navigational problem. But they had no choice; somehow they got new supplies aboard and survived grounding on a sandbar. Out at sea once more, they needed another five or six days to reach their intended destination.

The trip was star-crossed. Soon Johnny and Harry were soaking wet, sitting on a beach, glimpsing through the dark night the surf pounding their shipwrecked *Rose Marie* to pieces and washing their sacks of whisky bottles out to sea. The two salvaged what they could of the liquor, cached it, then sold it to some fishermen who said they would collect it later and pay then. Two nervous nights later, the fishermen finally showed at a rendezvous, but still did not hand over any payment. The next day, while Johnny and Harry were still in hiding, the cache was hijacked. Then they were arrested as they tried to pick up some money that would enable them to get back to Victoria. Finally set free, they hightailed it back to Canada.

Unlucky though it was, Johnny Schnarr's first venture into rum-running did not scare him out of the business. For two years, he worked running another man's boat, then he struck out on his own. In time, he became one of the biggest and best independent liquor smugglers operating out of Victoria, running loads of whisky for himself or for the big boys who owned the liquor conglomerates. When he wanted money to buy or build a better boat, CEC was happy to lend him the funds. After all, he was one of their best runners.

US Customs and the Coast Guard could be a problem,

but the biggest challenge was the sea. On one trip, a gale blew up as they were off Anacortes, in Juan de Fuca Strait. Water smashing onto the deck leaked into the ocean compartment, and the engine stalled. "We were immediately being driven towards a sheer rock wall that rose straight up out of the water," recounted Schnarr. "I dropped the anchor right away, but I knew it wouldn't hold for long against that wind." Faced with abandoning the boat, Schnarr could only wait and hope as the wind pushed them closer to the cliffs. "The thunder of the waves beating against that wall was deafening. We were close enough that the boat was surrounded by a sea of greenish-white foam. Then suddenly the wind died as quickly as it had come up." The boat and the men in her were safe. "Lucky, I guess," wrote Schnarr, and that might have been his watchword for the rest of his rum-running life.

The Coast Guard and US Customs got bigger, faster boats, but so did Schnarr, who turned out to be an expert at building boats and using his skills to retrofit airplane engines to them when others were unable to do so. Blessed with excellent night vision, he frequently evaded Coast Guard and customs boats. On the one occasion when he let others run his boat, they came under machine-gun fire from the Coast Guard and ran the boat up onto the shore. That finished that particular boat, and he never delegated the captain's job again.

If the men he was due to meet did not show, or if he felt delivery was unsafe, he stashed his liquor on one of the small islands in the San Juans, for pickup later. Aboard *Miss Victoria* and *Miss Victoria II*, *Moonbeam*, *Kitnayakwa* and *Revuocnav* (Vancouver backwards, to make the name harder to remember), Schnarr made hundreds of smuggling runs over more than 10 years. He once even delivered to a Coast Guard cutter when the captain took it out, off duty, for a personal load of booze. He made his trips mainly in winter when detection was more difficult in the long nights. He motored across the strait and up and down Puget Sound, hiding from pursuers in fog and dark. Thoroughly frustrated by his skills, US Customs posted a $25,000 reward for the capture of one of his boats.

Two days before the end of Prohibition, the king of Vancouver Island smugglers made his last run, 250 cases from Victoria to Seattle. Summing up, he said he had enjoyed his work, making some 400 runs, landing in 36 different spots along the Washington coastline and never missing rendezvous locations that he had often been shown only on a map. He landed liquor worth at least four million dollars, though at the end he had just $10,000 in the bank, a large sum for those times, but little enough for his risks. He had to have been lucky, he said, but through skill and good judgment, he also had made his own luck.

Hijacking and Murder
Many an account of the rum-running years makes them sound like fun and games—smugglers against police and

customs agents, sailing by night and bribing by day. Let the eastern United States deal with the gangs, their violence and their involvement with prostitution and other crimes. On the West Coast, things were more civilized. At one point, West Coast rum-runners even got together to work out their business ethics, famously declaring that they would have absolutely nothing to do with the evil business of smuggling drugs. Even when US Customs got faster boats and guns with more firepower, death or even injury to someone from either side was rare.

However, there were exceptions. Some rum-runners were hijacked by those who brought their boats alongside with seemingly peaceful intentions but then pulled their guns and took the load. Vancouver rum-runner Charlie Boys was looking for his rendezvous point on shore in Puget Sound when he was overtaken by a bigger, faster boat. Three armed men boarded his boat, announced they were officers of the law and that Boys was under arrest; they relieved him of some $3,000 in cash. Boys was taken aboard the larger boat, delivered to shore and shoved into a car. Not long after, he was shoved out again, sans boat, sans liquor, sans cash, sans everything, hijacked and deceived.

Other cases were less amusing. In September of 1924, the wooden freighter *Beryl G* disappeared at sea with 240 cases of whisky below decks. The next day, the lightkeeper at Turn Point Island at the northern end of Puget Sound saw the ship drifting with the tide. He and another man

The *Beryl G*, shown here in Victoria, was at the centre of the most sensational rum-running case on the West Coast. She was found adrift with her crew missing; eventually three men were sentenced to hang for their murders. BC ARCHIVES B-06106

rowed out to the ship, but there was no one aboard. Dinner remained half-eaten on the galley table. Spatters of blood patterned the floor and the deck. The boat was a mess.

Beryl G's captain, William Gillis, and his 18-year-old son, Bill, were nowhere to be found. No liquor remained in the *Beryl G*'s hold. Had hijackers taken the cargo and killed the crew? Rumours swirled around the docks at Victoria and Port Townsend. Informers, among them the rum-runner who had arranged for the ship to bring liquor to the United States, finally told all they knew. After many turnings and dead ends, the trail of rumour and names casually dropped into conversation led to four Americans with connections to liquor smuggling and sale.

Police finally broke one of the men, who confessed that though he had had little to do with the crime, he knew what had happened. On his evidence, the Canadian government was able to get the other three men extradited for trial. One was found in Seattle; another showed up in New Orleans, on the lam from the northwest. The third was discovered working the boats in New York City. All three were eventually extradited to Canada, though it took months to get the third back over the border. Meanwhile, two of the men, Harry Sowash and Owen Baker, went on trial in Victoria.

The witnesses disagreed over who had done what, but the outcome was clear. In the midst of hijacking the *Beryl G* and its cargo, the hijackers had shot the father and killed the son with a blunt object. The two bodies were handcuffed together and attached to a rope. One of the men slashed the bodies with a knife so that they would sink. Then he set the *Beryl G* adrift and towed the bodies out to sea with the hijackers' boat, dropping the line once they were in deep water.

The bodies were never recovered, but the testimony was enough to convict Sowash and Baker. They were sentenced to death. The third man lost his battle against extradition and was also tried and sentenced to hang. Two were hanged on January 14, 1926; the last to go to trial had his sentence commuted to life imprisonment.

The Biggest Fish

And then there was the biggest fish of all. Roy Olmstead was just 33 years old when he was promoted to the rank of lieutenant in the Seattle Police Force. Strong and intelligent, he seemed to have a fine policing career ahead of him—until he discovered how much money could be made rum-running by someone who could avoid the foolish mistakes and lack of organization he saw from amateurs engaged in the trade.

Olmstead promptly made a mistake of his own, running into a trap set by agents of the Prohibition Bureau. The agents captured 10 men, including another police officer, and about 100 cases of whisky, but Olmstead escaped. The agents had identified him, though, and he was ordered by his bosses to surrender. Tried and convicted, he was fined $500 and summarily tossed out of the police force.

No matter—rum-running seemed like a more profitable career than police work. Within a year or two, Olmstead was running more than 100 cases of liquor out of Victoria and into Seattle every day. He employed bookkeepers to keep track of shipments and money, warehousemen to look after liquor, drivers and mechanics for the cars and trucks, and lawyers to look after his interests and those of any employee who was caught. He owned a plethora of boats, trucks and cars.

Rum-running wasn't Olmstead's only business. He ran a radio and telephone company with his second wife, Elise, who read children's stories over the air. Agents speculated, though no proof was found, that the stories included coded messages for the rum-running fleet.

Dry agents badly wanted to stop Olmstead. Late in 1924, they raided the Olmstead house. Surprisingly, they found not a drop of liquor in the house. They had used informants to get the information they needed about Olmstead, but it seemed that information was a two-way street. Olmstead later confessed that he had bribed large numbers of people, from police to customs inspectors to dry agents to warehouse and dock men, to keep his business running.

Agents did, however, find incriminating documents in the house and had pages of transcripts from a wiretap they had installed on Olmstead's telephone. They charged Olmstead and 89 others with various violations of the National Prohibition Act and with conspiracy. It took a year for the case to come to court; meanwhile, 43 defendants had either disappeared or turned state's evidence. Olmstead and 20 others were convicted, but Elise was acquitted. Olmstead was sentenced to four years in the penitentiary and fined $8,000, surely a small portion of the profits he had made. He appealed up to the US Supreme Court, arguing that use of wiretap evidence was unconstitutional. He lost. The king of the bootleggers was in jail. By the time he was released in 1931, Prohibition was on its way out.

In any case, Olmstead was no longer interested in rum-running. Converted to Christian Science while in jail, he now believed that liquor was destructive to man and society.

He got a job as a furniture salesman and spent many of his non-working hours visiting jails. With his wife battling for him, he was granted a full presidential pardon in 1935, and the $8,000 in fines plus court costs were returned to him. Elise later divorced him, claiming desertion, and Olmstead spent the rest of his life working full time with Christian Science as a counsellor, Sunday-school teacher and prison visitor.

Rum Row

SS *Quadra* steamed out of Vancouver harbour one moon-lit night in 1924. Originally built as a lighthouse tender for the Canadian government in 1891, her duties had included policing the fishing and sealing fleets off the northwest coast. But then she came down in the world: she sank after a colli-sion with another ship and was refloated to work as an ore carrier. There was plenty of room below decks, though, for more profitable cargo, so workers for the Canadian Mexican Shipping Company loaded aboard 22,000 cases of liquor and a large quantity of beer, consigned, according to the ship's manifest, for Ensenada, Mexico.

Quadra was barely into Juan de Fuca Strait when she hove to and waited for several launches that raced out from the opposite shore. Each captain presented half of a dollar bill with a liquor list written on it, which was matched with a half bill by the supercargo on *Quadra*. Identification duly made, each order was transferred from the larger ship to the smaller boat, and the boats made for the American shore. At Astoria, off the Oregon coast, the process was repeated.

Quadra was scheduled to make a similar stop off San Francisco, but a storm forced her to heave to for a week. She was also running out of liquor, so the captain took her up beside the five-masted wooden schooner *Malahat*, the queen of the liquor fleet, which often carried 50,000 cases of fine liquors. Somehow, she hit the *Malahat*. Busy stuffing mattresses into her side to keep her afloat as they drifted away, the crew failed to notice the approach of a Coast Guard cutter.

Once they noticed, some of the crew tried to slip away in a launch. The cutter's crew fired a shot, and the launch stopped. Facing up to reality, *Quadra*'s crew went quietly. The ship was seized and taken into San Francisco harbour where the main crew members were arrested and charged with various offences. The company that owned the ship fought the charges, but the American government used delay as a weapon. Every day that *Quadra* was kept at the dock was a day not spent smuggling. By now in a sorry state, *Quadra* finally was sold at auction.

Such were the hazards of Rum Row. Though many rum-running stories are about small boats that took liquor from British Columbia along the coast, the real money was in the larger ships that steamed south with thousands of cases on board, standing off the coasts of Oregon and California beyond the territorial limit, while smaller American boats dashed to and fro.

These mother ships—*Malahat, Coal Harbour, Stadacona, Mogul, Prince Albert, Hurry On, Lillehorn, Hurry Home* and *Quadra*—lined up on Rum Row, each ship a floating warehouse of whisky, rum, champagne, gin and beer. The men aboard had backgrounds as varied as the ships they sailed on; what they had in common was their desire to make their wages. Sworn to drink nothing from the moment the ship left port, they were well looked after by the ship's owners. If the ship was captured and the crew arrested, their bail or fines would be paid, as well as their wages for any time spent in jail.

Charles Hudson, marine superintendent for CEC, had no doubt that he was working for the good of Vancouver and Canada in his job. Vancouver, he told an interviewer years later, was in a depression in the early 1920s, and it was rum-running that helped reverse the downward spiral. "The tremendous moneys paid out to industry in Vancouver were never known by the average citizen. We spent a fabulous amount of money building boats; purchasing and overhauling engines; buying food and supplies for our ships; using the ship-yards for overhaul and in wages for the crew and fuel." Many people, he said, thought of rum-running as a piratical trade, filled with shooting, killing, hijacking and boozing. But it was, in fact, a sane money-making proposition.

It was also filled with adventure. Hudson wouldn't stay ashore and supervise; instead he signed on as captain of *Coal Harbour*. On her final trip, she was well outside territorial limits when the Coast Guard sent a shot across her bows and tried to arrest her. Hudson demurred, but the Coast Guard managed to get two men aboard, then seven, then finally a dozen. Outgunned, Hudson gave in, though loudly proclaiming the ship was more than 26 miles (42 kilometres) offshore, well beyond the legitimate patrol area for the US Coast Guard. A 1924 treaty specified that the United States would be permitted to arrest ships suspected of smuggling liquor only if the ship was within the distance it could reach from shore within one hour—an almost impossible rule to measure and enforce. The case went to court but was dismissed when the skipper of the Coast Guard cutter was found to have lied about *Coal Harbour*'s position. The skipper was also dismissed and later found guilty of perjury.

The Coast Guard would not be restrained long by legalities. Several ships were commandeered well outside the limit and then left at the dock in San Francisco while the legal arguments went on. Sometimes the seizure was upheld and the ship retained by the American government; sometimes it was not. But it mattered little, for as long as the ship was in the United States, it wasn't out on the seas, running liquor into the country.

The End of Prohibition

By 1933, the American government had spent some $140 million trying to enforce the National Prohibition Act, with only about $65 million coming back in fines and judgments. Some 2,000 agents and investigators were trying to stop people from drinking and smuggling drink into the United States. But people continued to imbibe, and smuggling was an ever bigger and more organized business. The noble experiment had become an ignoble failure. In December 1933, Prohibition was repealed.

There were still some penalties to be paid by the big boys of the smuggling trade. Henry Reifel, for example, visited the United States in 1934 with his son. They were promptly charged with smuggling liquor into the United States during Prohibition and had to pay $200,000 in bail in order to go home. They forfeited the bail when they did not return for their arraignment in court. The case did not, in fact, ever come to trial, for the Reifels paid the American government half a million dollars in back taxes and fines.

In one last irony or insult, authorities were still concerned about liquor smuggling throughout the 1930s. But this time it was the smuggling of whisky, rum, champagne and beer into Canada from the United States, as legitimate brewers and distillers in the United States were able to price their products much lower than competing products made in Canada.

In the annals of West Coast smuggling, rum-running occupies a place of its own as a far larger enterprise than all the other smuggling that preceded it. It would not be matched in size and impact until BC bud came on the scene. Today, marijuana smuggling from British Columbia to the United States and drug smuggling into British Columbia make rum-running look like an amateur operation.

Bibliography

Books

Bancroft, Hubert Howe. *History of British Columbia*. Los Angeles: A.L. Bancroft & Company, 1887.

Fahey, Edmund. *Rum Road to Spokane*. Missoula: University of Montana, 1972.

Greene, Hilda. *Personality Ships of British Columbia*. West Vancouver, BC: Marine Tapestry Publications, 1969.

Kahn, David. *The Codebreakers*. New York: Simon and Schuster, 1996.

Norton, Wayne and Naomi Miller, eds. *The Forgotten Side of the Border*. Kamloops: Plateau Press, 1998.

Parker, Marion and Bob Tyrell. *Rumrunner: The Life and Times of Johnny Schnarr*. Victoria: Orca Books, 1988.

Richardson, David. *Pig War Islands*. Eastsound: Orcas Publishing Company, 1990.

Schneider, Stephen. *Iced: The Story of Organized Crime in Canada*. Toronto: John Wiley and Sons, 2009.

Wilson, Gary. *Honky-Tonk Town: Havre, Montana's Lawless Era*. Guilford, CT: Globe Pequot Press, 2006.

Articles and Reports

Cameron, James D. "Canada's Struggle with Illegal Entry on Its West Coast." *BC Studies* 146 (Summer 2005): 37–62. Also available online at http://ojs.library.ubc.ca/index.php/bcstudies/article/view/1757/1802.

Bibliography

Griffith, Sarah M. "Border Crossings: Race, Class and Smuggling in Pacific Coast Chinese Immigrant Society." *Western Historical Quarterly* 35, no. 4 (Winter 2004): 473–92.

Mackenzie King, W.L. *The Need for the Suppression of the Opium Traffic in Canada*. Ottawa: Department of Labour, 1908. Also available online at www.archive.org/stream/reportbywlmacken00canarich#page/n1/mode/2up.

Montgomery, Gary. "Booze Across the Border." *Tobacco Plains Journal* 6, no. 2 (September 1997).

Ralph, Julian. "The Chinese Leak." *Harper's New Monthly Magazine*, March 1891.

Newspapers

British Colonist (Daily British Colonist, Daily Colonist) (Victoria)
New York Times
Oregonian (Portland)
Vancouver Daily World
Vancouver Sun

Websites

Chinese in Northwest America Research Committee. www.cinarc.org.

Colonial Despatches: The Colonial Despatches of Vancouver Island and British Columbia 1846–1871. http://bcgenesis.uvic.ca/index.htm.

Index

140

Index

Acknowledgements

Smuggling on North America's west coast has a long and complex tradition, one with a plethora of tales and legends, some of them true and some owing more to the teller's imagination than to verifiable fact. Sorting out truth from fantasy has been a fascinating task, and I owe much to those writers and historians who tackled that task before me.

The books and writers to whom I owe a debt are listed in the bibliography. Much material is now online, in the form of reports, essays, newspapers and family histories, among other sources. I thank those who took the time and expended the energy required to create these digital resources.

I am particularly grateful to all those in the distant past and up to the present who loved good smuggling stories. I know that today's smuggling of drugs and people causes untold harm, and I do not mean to downplay that harm. The West Coast smugglers of the past, however—with some notable exceptions—seem to have caused less destruction, and though I do not glorify their actions, I present their stories with that in mind.

I thank Heritage House managing editor Vivian Sinclair for the opportunity to write this book, and editor Lesley Reynolds, who once more did a fine job of sorting out inconsistencies and restraining wordiness.

About the Author

Rosemary Neering has been writing about the Pacific Northwest for more than three decades. She is the author of many books on the area, including *British Columbia Bizarre: Stories, Whimsies, Facts, and a Few Outright Lies from Canada's Wacky West Coast*; *Down the Road: Journeys through Small-Town British Columbia*; *Wild West Women: Travellers, Adventurers and Rebels*; and *A Traveller's Guide to Historic British Columbia*, as well as *The Pig War* in the Amazing Stories series. She is fascinated by the offbeat and lesser-known stories of the region. Rosemary lives in Victoria with her partner, Joe Thompson, and her cat, but makes frequent forays into the backwoods.

More Great Books in the Amazing Stories Series

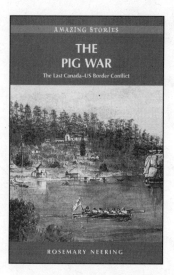

The Pig War

The Last Canada–US Border Conflict

Rosemary Neering

(ISBN 978-1-926936-01-7)

On May 15, 1859, an American settler on San Juan Island shot a pig belonging to the Hudson's Bay Company. This seemingly insignificant act almost triggered an all-out war between Britain and the United States on the northwest coast of North America. At stake was control of the strategically located San Juan Islands, and as both sides mustered their forces, conflict seemed inevitable. This lively account of the border dispute now known as the Pig War traces the events that led to the standoff in the San Juans and brings to life the memorable characters who played leading roles in the drama.

Visit www.heritagehouse.ca to see the entire list of books in this series.